Surviving The
High School Jungle

Surviving The High School Jungle

An Inside Look at Teaching in the Modern Age

Mary Ann Revell

iUniverse, Inc.
New York   Bloomington

Surviving the High School Jungle

An Inside Look at Teaching in the Modern Age

Copyright © 2008 by Mary Ann Revell

iUniverse books may be ordered through booksellers or by contacting:

iUniverse
1663 Liberty Drive
Bloomington, IN 47403
www.iuniverse.com
1-800-Authors (1-800-288-4677)

ISBN: 978-0-595-52833-2 (pbk)
ISBN: 978-0-595-51696-4 (cloth)
ISBN: 978-0-595-62886-5 (ebk)

Printed in the United States of America

iUniverse rev. date: 11/17/08

To Charles, who helped bring the stories of these young
people to life, while making my life complete.

Introduction

Some years ago in a small, quiet American suburb, two high school students murdered twelve of their classmates, a teacher, and themselves. The setting for this tragedy was the beautiful, peaceful Rocky Mountains, so no one wanted to believe such evil could be incubated there. And people were afraid of this unknown—could it happen again? Will our children, grandchildren, or other young people we love be victims?

"What goes on in these schools?" now everyone wants to know. After thirty years in the education business, still there are days I wonder if I made the best choices for my life. Sometimes I wonder if anyone can answer this question. I've witnessed much—maybe not mass murder—but I've been roughed up by drug dealers and cursed at more times than I care to count. And I have cried, for better or worse, more often than I should have.

At a faculty meeting, another teacher told us about a kindergarten teacher who was pregnant. She passed out in class, and when she came to, she looked up to see several angelic faces towering over her. The little ones said, "Is she dead?" "Can we go to recess?" and "I bet we get a substitute." Since all of us were high school teachers, we could not resist speculating on what we would wake up to if we passed out. All we could hope for was that they would not trample all over our bodies as they escaped through the door.

Young people use poor judgment and make mistakes—plenty of them. Often they believe that no one else has ever been tempted to steal or fallen in love for the first time. When the experience bowls them over, they are blinded to all good sense. Some recover, such as the young man I sent into my back office to retrieve a paper. While he was there, he helped himself to a hat belonging to my student assistant. Although wealthy enough to afford any hat, he sensed an opportunity, and he took it. When confronted and threatened with exposure, he confessed and apologized. His greatest lament was his concern that I would not "like him again."

"Sam," I said, "you kids do lots of stupid things. At least you made good on it. Try to learn something from your mistake."

Sam visited me often after he left my class, so I guessed that he was keeping his lifeline open to test whether or not he was truly forgiven. I forgave him. The youngsters have taught me to judge compassionately. Teachers need empathy with others in order to succeed.

Beginnings

From the second grade, when Sister Mary Madonna RSM handed me a pointer and a reading book and told me to go teach the bluebirds (the slow boys' group), I knew that I was meant to teach. Sister was overwhelmed with fifty baby boomers in her little classroom and needed help. After months of drills, focus, and empathy, those slow boys read just like the others. And some years later as a preteen, I learned a teacher's compassion from a fellow student, Virginia.

Surviving sixth grade seemed challenging enough for any girl, without the additional burdens of being overweight, unattractive, and poor. We were all poor, but Virginia's poverty made the remainder of us seem well-off by comparison. She spent the majority of her school day being ignored by all the other cool girls in Sr. Mary Augustine's sixth and seventh grade class. But while preparing to choose the "Mary Mother of Jesus Queen" for the month of April, someone not only thought of Virginia, but nominated her. All the girls voted, then Sister religiously counted the ballots, stood before the class, and announced, "the Queen for April will be—pause, pause, pause—Virginia!"

We stood, applauded, and faced her, expecting the usual, "Oh my, oh my." But this month was strange. No tears of joy gushed down her full cheeks. Tears of deep anguish flowed instead, just like the River Jordan. She wept and sobbed so loudly that the sixth and seventh grade boys next door probably wondered what all those girls were up to now.

After gaining some composure, she stared imploringly into the nun's eyes and said something that I have never forgotten.

She bellowed, "Sister, I cannot do this. It should be an honor for a girl who is pretty, popular, and smart—someone like Julianne." We all encouraged Virginia to accept the crown and be "Queen" for the month of April. She reluctantly placed the crown on her head, smiled, and just beamed.

I often recalled that event in the afternoon of 1961 as I made decisions every day in the classroom. I tried to be aware of the Virginias who were everywhere and be on their side.

In the spring of 1970, I interned at Waite High School on the East Side of Toledo, Ohio. Only in those days we called ourselves "student teachers." The school had two claims to fame; the singer Teresa Brewer, who graduated from Waite High; and Tony Packo's, the restaurant made famous by the popular television series, M*A*S*H, that was located right around the corner. Lunches there with the rest of the faculty are about all I remember of those days. But even if I had garnered anything from the experience, it would not have prepared me for the outrageous fortunes that teaching would bring.

Since 1970 I have taught something to someone, somewhere all across the country. Most people, who pass through the delicate years of public school, do so with minimal damage. Some never recover. Here are the stories of both.

Neglect

"Shall I compare thee to a summer's day…"
William Shakespeare

As part of their graduation requirement, seniors had to complete a portfolio/project that included the assignment of writing a first-hand account of their most vivid childhood memory. When conceiving this exercise, I foolishly mused that their papers would be about "Fluffy," the cuddly kitten that Daddy surprised them with on their fifth birthday, or seeing Mommy drive home in their brand-new shiny green Ford Explorer. Instead, one of the first papers was written by a dark-haired beauty who explicitly remembered keeping Daddy busy in the living room the day he came home early. Why did she occupy Daddy? Because Mommy had her boyfriend in the bedroom, and they needed time to skedaddle him out the back door. When I asked what her parents would think when they read her account, she had no trouble saying, "As if they would ever read anything of mine!"

So the next year, I carefully announced that the memory should focus on something happy and joyful that they experienced as a child—something their grandmothers could read to the pope. I desired them to think back on happier times, not dwell on the morbid or painful. The high school English class was not the appropriate place for psychoanalysis; we had professionals on staff paid to help with those problems. One paper touched me so much that I cried, especially when I recalled how I had emphasized that they were to focus on the "happiest day of their young lives."

Jason

Christmas Eve with a No-show Mommy

What did our Jason choose for his "happiest" day? He wrote about the one and only day he met his father. Jason recalled, "He looked so tall in his blue jeans. I was looking right at his belt. My mother left me with him for about one hour, and he showed me all of his medals from Vietnam. I was proud that he was my father. He said that he would not be able to see me too much, and then he shook my hand and told me to take care of my mother. He also said that he would always love me. I never saw him again."

If God erred in creating the universe, certainly the most blatant consequence is the fact that sex has something to do with parenthood. A sperm and egg meeting creates a beautiful person, like Jason, but the sperm and egg donors do not have a clue as to what they have done. Since his adored fantasy father was nowhere to be found, Jason was left with a drug-addicted, selfish woman for his only parent. She managed to give him something resembling care for a number of years, until she met up with a new boyfriend—her drug supplier. Unfortunately, he wanted no part of two teenage "bastard" children, so mommy threw the boys out on the street. Since his half-brother knew who and where his father was, he went off to a new life in Arkansas. Jason, however, had only a vague memory of a Vietnam vet to call father. So he moved from one day to another and from one house to another.

As his teacher, I noticed that Jason came to class disinterested, slept regularly at his desk, and often tried me by doing exactly the opposite of his assignments. If they were supposed to work in groups, he wanted to be alone. If they were supposed to relax, close their eyes, and visualize, Jason sat straight as a board and stared right at me. If we were reading "Macbeth," he wanted to read about soldiers, as long as it was what he was not supposed to do.

Finally in November he smiled and even communicated some positive thoughts to me and a couple of the girls who minded everyone's business. He asked if we knew of a nice restaurant to take a girl. Well, naturally we assumed that Jason had a girlfriend and things were finally beginning to look up for him.

Janice thought that the Olive Garden might do, but I and another girl said that it was "too ordinary." We offered some suggestions of quieter places with dimmer lighting.

"Have you known her long?" I tried to pry more details out of him.

"What kind of food does she like?" Janice asked.

Jason remained secretive to the end and gave us no clue as to the reason for the rendezvous. Jason was happy that day, happier than I had ever seen him. I delighted in his forgetting his troubles, and just being a teen.

Christmas came and I focused on my own dear ones and completely forgot the restaurant story. That January, I passed one of Jason's other teachers and asked Paul how he was doing in psychology. Paul said that Jason would pass, but not by much.

"Did he ask you about a restaurant before the holidays?" Paul inquired.

"Yeah, how did you know about that?" I asked, surprised that Jason wanted advice from a bachelor. "We thought he wanted the female perspective," I joked.

"Do you know who his date was supposed to be?" Paul looked disgusted.

I knew from his tone that this was not going to be a good story, especially the "supposed to be" part, but I replied, "Some little cutie?"

"Not even close," Paul spoke slowly. He explained that Jason had been on the streets for weeks, staying with this and that friend, until no one wanted him. With the holidays coming, Jason telephoned his mother, hoping to get an invitation for Christmas Day. She accepted his dinner date.

Jason hitched a ride to the restaurant and told his friend that he was meeting his mother and she would give him a ride back home. Jason sat alone at the table for three hours. She never showed up. There was no opportunity for her to tell him, "Have a Merry Christmas, son."

I obviously was not with Jason when he sat at his table and looked around eagerly for his mom. I did not see him stare each time a woman walked past his table. No one noticed his face, bright when he still believed she would appear, crestfallen as hope faded, and finally ashen with despair.

When the second semester began, an angel came to give Jason a second chance. He was failing his classes and in danger of losing his dream of joining the Marines in June. A generous family took Jason in, and encouraged him to get his grades to where he would at least be able to graduate.

"I've done the numbers, Mrs. Revell. The only way he walks out of high school in time to join up is to manage a B in senior English," his guardian told me matter-of-factly.

"Well, sir," I began, "a bright student would have difficulty getting a D minus to a B by May. And Jason is only average on a very good day. Mathematically it's not there."

Instead of bribing, threatening, or cajoling me (as several desperate parents have in the past), he simply restated the facts. Jason had to have a B in order for the Marines to accept him. If he wasn't able to go into the military, no one knew the alternative.

So I offered a proposal. "If Jason does B+ work from now until graduation, I will pencil in the B column on his grade sheet. That's the most I can stretch my professional conscience," I replied. Thinking there was no way that Jason could achieve this standard, I also suggested that he contact the administration and try to get the boy moved to an "easier" teacher. I was fairly certain that another English teacher would be willing to help.

"No, we wouldn't ask. Anyway, Jason wants to finish the year with you," he replied. I expected a major butt-kissing session to follow, but actually that was all he said; we left it at that.

Jason woke up in English class, smiled more, and even came in early just to talk. I couldn't believe that he was the same young man. He even volunteered to do cartwheels down the center aisle of the class for extra credit. Despite saying, "That will not be necessary," when I looked the other way, I caught sight of him cart wheeling down the center of my classroom. Jason was able to bring his grade up to a low B.

Jason did graduate, and his "adopted" family invited all of his teachers to his farewell bash. Jason did not naturally take to the role of "guest of honor." I wondered if he had ever experienced the euphoria of being the center of attention. Had he ever had a birthday party at McDonald's? Did he wear a funny hat, eat French fries, and listen to all the other kids sing "Happy Birthday" to him? Probably not. Now a house full of people, neighbors, teachers, friends, and little kids were bringing presents just for him.

Jason cracked under the pressure. He frenetically tried to get his mom on the phone—no number, no forwarding address, no mom. After the younger, half-brother gave him a few leads, he seemed encouraged. But ultimately she was not found. He cried. He bawled in my arms.

"I have to talk to her before I leave. Just a couple of minutes, that's all. She doesn't even know I graduated," Jason sobbed. Those were the first tears I ever witnessed him shed over her. We sat together on the big double swing, looking out on the lake, but I avoided his eyes. I had no answers for Jason. All I could do it tell him I loved him, and that others loved him too. His Mom was sick, and I did not know if she would ever get well.

That Monday, Jason left for the Marines. He promised to visit his old classroom wearing his shiny starched uniform. I hoped he would keep his word and the double picture frame that I gave to him as a graduation present. My picture was on one side and I asked him to put a picture on the other side of someone who made him smile.

Just after Christmas of the next year, I saw Jason again. He was wearing his shiny starched uniform and looked more like a man than ever before. He told me how tough basic training was, but that he loved every minute of it. I didn't ask about his mom. He did tell me that he was not so sure that he wanted to make the Marines his life. Jason said that he had begun to compose poetry in his spare time, and that he might even want to finish college and be an English teacher. I believe he meant it.

Amanda

Dilated at Her Desk

Some kids make a "monumental" impact on teachers; some are barely remembered. One advantage to living in today's economy is that so many waiters, hostesses, and sales clerks wear nametags. So when I saw my former students in the grocery store, or they waited on me at the Golden Corral, I could call them by name regardless of how well I remembered them. Amanda was well on her way to being designated to what I call the "Hope she is wearing a name tag" alumni. Then she took a radical turn to the "I'll never forget that one" category.

During the last class period of the day just before spring break, Amanda was writhing in obvious pain. Her head was lying directly on her desk pad and she rolled it violently back and forth. Amanda, a straight A student, never talked to anyone, and did her work meticulously.

"Do you want me to write a pass to the clinic for you?" I asked her tentatively.

"No, I'm okay," she managed to spit out.

I considered insisting, but realized that by the time someone had gotten there, it would be time to leave anyway—she would get home just as quickly. What I learned later was that there was absolutely no one for her to call, at least not anyone that the school would let her go with. She would need to be released to a parent or guardian, and Amanda lacked anything vaguely resembling either.

Class proceeded unremarkably and then we all went home.

Third period the next day, Aline asked me if I had heard about Amanda.

"No, is she terribly ill?" I cringed to think that I had not immediately called 911 or offered something to alleviate her distress.

"She's not sick. She had a baby yesterday," said little Aline like she was announcing the lunch menu.

"A BABY!" I cried aloud. Amanda was in labor right there in the second desk, third row, left section from the front chalkboard. Having given birth to two children via "natural" myself, I knew what she was suffering right there in my Room 406.

"Did you know she was pregnant?" I asked Aline.

"No, nobody knew. She still doesn't want anyone to know. She's giving it away."

"Is she coming back to school?"

"Don't know."

A few weeks later Amanda officially withdrew from high school and was placed on a homebound program, which allowed incapacitated students to continue with their studies and graduate. I assumed that I would never see her again and even had trouble remembering what she looked like.

Two days before graduation, Amanda appeared in my room, much slimmer than I remembered her. But then I had only known her "with child."

After a big hug, we talked. She had given birth to a perfect 7 lb. 13 oz. girl a few hours after she left school. She rode home on a bus with "broken water" and four centimeters of dilation. Why? Why no prenatal care, no vitamins, no special diets, no joy, no sorrow, only terror?

I had to ask, "So why all the secrecy? Are your parents violent? Were you protecting the father? Did you fear disappointing them, public shame, or religious intolerance? What would drive an intelligent young lady to such extremes?"

"I've never met my dad. Until my mother was called to the Children's Hospital, I hadn't seen her in six months."

"Six months!" I must have sounded as surprised as I was, "So whom do you live with?"

"We live in the same house as my mother, but my sister and I pretty much take care of ourselves," she admitted.

"You have an older sister?" I asked.

"No, she's only a sophomore here."

"Is her father your step-father?" I'm still desperately trying to capture an image of this poor girl's life.

"No, she has a different father, but she never saw him either."

"So your mother has two different children with two different men, both of whom she had no relationship with. And you haven't actually laid eyes on her in six months. Have I got it right now?"

"Right, but it's not as horrible as it sounds. She's a social worker and she's very busy..."

"Whoa, you mean she's an educated professional and she didn't even know her own daughter was pregnant?" By this time I was visibly angry.

"Really, Mrs. Revell, she really loves me and we're very close—we just never see each other. She comes home late at night when I am already asleep, and on weekends, she is gone with her girlfriend—I mean partner." By then Amanda was in tears and could not go on.

Because she did not break any of her daughter's bones, this "child abuser" will never be arrested. She'll go about her business as a respected member of the community, although she is the most incipient type of child abuser. She simply ignored the fact that she gave birth to two beautiful girls who needed someone in their lives. And so the elder sister found a little attention and affection in the only person who knew that she was alive. At this point we changed the subject to baby Veronica and the daddy.

"Is this what you want for your daughter? No daddy, mom gone all the time?" Now the tears were flowing.

Naturally, Amanda said she wanted better for her child, but she knew the cycle often repeated. Baby Veronica would have no father in the home, no grandparents to speak of, and a mother who had just completed high school with aspirations of starting college. I skipped ahead mentally seventeen years in the future. I pictured the teenager Veronica sitting in classroom nine months pregnant writhing in pain, trying to understand the words:

> Shall I compare thee to a summer's day?
> Thou art more lovely and more temperate:
> Rough winds do shake the darling buds of May,
> And summer's lease hath all too short a date:

Metaphorical images are difficult to comprehend when you're four centimeters dilated.

Where Have All the Parents Gone?

So many of our kids don't have fathers living with them, but they do not forget that there is a father out there; he is just not living with them. It's tough on all of them, and the ones with unstable care-givers suffer even more. One quiet little girl in a sophomore honors class shared with us that her mother was in a mental institution. One of the therapies that her mother was undergoing was to keep a journal of her everyday thoughts. I was in no position to judge the therapeutic value of this exercise, but I let her read her mother's most private thoughts. As she read, I quickly realized that sharing these thoughts was not advisable, especially the parts about how the mother hated everyone—including her children.

Another fifteen-year-old was bragging to her classmates how her married "boyfriend" was twenty-nine years old. I could not resist the urge to interject my personal thoughts on the subject.

"There's no father in your house, is there?" I asked.

"Why no, Mrs. Revell. How did you know?" She seemed so surprised by my ESP.

"Because your father would kill him—or relieve him of some vital body parts—if he knew what was going on," I retorted. I observed in her eyes that there was plenty going on and no one around to stop it.

Ellissa

Daddy's Little Girl

When my students seemed determined to convince me that their fathers were the lowest scum on earth, I knew that they hurt the most. Ellissa's father was an irresponsible artist whose greatest fault was his inconsistency. He would show up, make all kinds of promises, and then disappear for months.

Her mother had great hopes for her only child, but she too seemed to be ungrounded. They moved from apartment to apartment when they could not pay the rent. Although Ellissa was bright, she barely made B's and C's in her classes. Meanwhile, her mother insisted that Ellissa would attend college if it killed her. There was no money and just mediocre grades, but mom never let Ellissa forget all her dreams for her only daughter.

"I hate him and I wish he would die," Ellissa would often say about her father.

"There has to be something good about the man, Ellissa. After all, he produced a beautiful, warm-hearted daughter like you." I tried to remind her that she was special and he was half of that. Later when she developed a chronic debilitating disease, Ellissa needed two parents, at least one good one. But there she was out of school for weeks at a time, with teachers giving her a hassle and no one to turn to. She gave so much and asked for so little. Her father could have had such a marvelous person in his life, if he had only tried.

Sarah

Prom Night Tears

Another lost little fatherless girl touched me particularly because she dated my only son. Sarah needed a stable male figure in her life. An immature sixteen-year-old boy could never fill the bill. She needed to know that her father loved her and cared enough to want to know how her life was going.

When Brad and Sarah went together to her junior prom, they posed for me in the family room. As I snapped picture after picture of her with the big corsage, and him in a tuxedo, tears filled my eyes.

"I wish your dads could see you now," I said as my eyes watered. And while I was only teary, Sarah broke right down into tears.

"Now you've done it," my son came at me belligerently, "Did you have to remind her of him?"

And so I have a girl bawling at the thought of her father not there, and a boy raising cane with me. All children need their parents; they just react differently when reminded of their abysmal loss.

Rose-Marie

Death Row Dad

Bubbly, bright, and outspoken are words that best described this young lady, who was torn between loving and despising her father. After mouthing "unprintable" adjectives to describe her dad, Rose-Marie admitted that most of what she knew of him originated with her mother. I frequently suggested that she acquaint herself with this person on her own terms. After she left high school, she eventually made contact with her father and began to be slightly more tolerant of him and his life choices.

Several years after her graduation, Rose-Marie reappeared in her old English classroom to tell me how well she was doing in college. The subject of "dad" came up in our conversation.

"I see him as much as I am allowed to now," she almost boasted.

"Why, are there restrictions?" I naively asked.

"Oh, he's on Death Row. But Mom and I are trying to get him a new trial—we're hopeful," she retorted as unemotionally as if he were a missionary in China.

How was it possible for a "Death Row" inmate to have a daughter as articulate and lovely as Rose-Marie? They were both fortunate that they reconciled before it was too late. Otherwise, Rose-Marie would have been resigned to a lifetime of questions and regret. And if dad has since been executed by the state, maybe he found some peace before he left her.

Prostitution

"Get thee to a Nunnery"
Hamlet

One of the many states that found me at the front of a classroom was Maryland where the taxpayers' dollars abounded. Much of the money went into the numerous military bases there, which spawned community colleges that served the soldiers/sailors and their families. I'm not sure if these older students learned anything from me, but I recall a great deal about them.

My very first adult education class was Speech 101, and I was nervous and curious about how I'd be accepted. My answer came immediately. A fifty-year-old woman bounced into the room, glared at me and said, "Don't take this personally, but college professors are supposed to be men with graying temples, not young girls." She immediately left, leaving me no time to rebut her. I was not a professor, just an instructor working the night classes that everyone else on staff had flatly rejected.

When I turned fifty so many years later, I felt inklings of wisdom that had accumulated in bits and pieces from trial and error. And it had taken a long time, like the first rain that falls on a hot asphalt roof. The initial droplets are immediately turned to steam and lost. Eventually, the cooling process takes hold, the next drops run off into a minor stream. As the pellets pound harder and harder, the accumulation grows into a river headed for the roof's edge. I'm still in the stream stage, but way ahead of the people of the 1960's who believed that anyone over 30 was out of touch with reality.

Exposure to people involved in the illegal trade of human flesh brought me into reality in a hurry. Yes, there are bona fide "Pimps & Whores" in schools. I have taught several.

The Pimp

"I'm too weary to do it any more."

I stayed seven years at the community college. Of the hundreds of students who passed my way, I recall one vividly. He was taking evening classes to qualify for a better position in life than his current one, which was a pimp. School teachers normally do not count pimps among their myriad students, or at least, we are not aware of their occupations outside of the classroom. For a persuasive speech assignment, I recommended that they choose something with which they were comfortably familiar. The pimp decided to write about his job. Surprisingly, he didn't look like the stereotypical pimp—no hat or big-daddy fur coat. As a matter of fact, he looked like an insurance or real estate agent.

After class, I had to badger him for more information about his salient past. His mild manner convinced me that he was more a victim of life circumstances, not someone who had actively chosen to barter in human flesh. Although the money was excellent and the fringe benefits unmentionable, he had two major reasons for wanting to quit the business. The first reason was that one of the girls had blessed his life with a three-year-old son for whom he was now the only supporting parent. He worshiped his son, and naturally wanted a world for him not limited by having a father who was a pimp. That response was the obvious, Hollywood-type answer I could have figured out for myself. But the second reason surprised me and I've never forgotten it.

He said, "I'm too weary to do it any more. You see, the only way to be really successful in this business is to find a stable of lonely fillies who become completely dependent on you. Each girl has to be convinced that she is my special one and true love, or she will not perform well. Women will do anything for true love, even giving their bodies to other men."

Prostitutes use sex to get the love they crave. The pimp met their needs physically and emotionally for years, but now he was drained. Selling real estate would be easier for him.

Years later, after ten years in the public schools, I discovered the secret to good teaching. I became the mother/pimp, there to scold, correct, direct, and convince each and every person that he or she was my "special" one. Small things made all the difference. They welcomed a hug when they regressed to their childhood, sobbing because their missed a mom or a dad left behind in the islands. Sometimes they needed to believe that their concerns made sense to someone beside themselves. Most of all, I learned to listen—ceasing all the scurrying and just focusing on what they said. Listening worked miracles with the teens.

Romeka

Bikini in a Black Raincoat

While teaching eighth grade, prostitution reared its ugly head again. Although she was sixteen years old, Romeka was still a middle school student. Slow-witted to begin with and coming from the most impossible of family situations, she never had a prayer. Her grades were deplorable, attendance minimal, and future dismal. When I checked with the guidance department, I was informed that her mother could not receive welfare checks if the daughter did not meet minimum attendance standards. Her fellow students were more informative and less kind. They said she turned tricks in the red-light district in the south part of town. Her "method of operation" was wearing a bikini covered with a black raincoat. Romeka's mother occasionally dropped her off at school after a late shift of work. Everyone assumed it would have been difficult for her to study after she had been "working" all night. I reported the situation to the administrators, but nothing changed.

Blue Eyes from Ohio

"He has the legal right to take him."

I encountered another case of child exploitation during my first year at high school. While assigned the odious task of dealing with parents in the attendance office, an attractive blue-eyed blond 15-year-old boy sat across the counter from me waiting for his parents to come and get him. He was being suspended for fighting on campus, and he could not leave alone. Someone from home would have to claim him. Through the door walked a thin black man, about thirty years old with shiny silk clothes, long curly hair, and more makeup than I ever wore.

He ambled over to the counter and in an effeminate voice whimpered, "I'm here for the boy. My name is Michael Jackson, and I'm his guardian."

My knees gave way. What business would this strange person have with one of our adolescent boys? After I asked him to have a seat, I charged in to see an administrator.

"There's a Michael Jackson here to take the boy," I tried to remain calm.

"We have to let him," answered Frazier. He was well acquainted with Mr. Jackson and needed no more details.

"And why do we 'have to'?" I asked.

"It's because Mr. Jackson is his legal guardian. People downtown know all about the situation—he has the legal right to take him. Let him go," was the tart reply.

I studied their bizarre relationship as they walked out the door together. The younger boy seemed to genuinely like the mommy-man. Or maybe the troubled young boy was just relieved to be out of school again.

Not being able to leave it at that, I headed to the student files in the guidance department. What I learned was incredible. The records went back to Ohio and indicated that blue-eyes was initially in the custody of his natural father, with no mention of the mother. The father moved to Alabama and married. When that relationship soured, the stepmother then assumed responsibility of the little no-name boy. Four years later, just about at puberty, the stepmother turned blue-eyes over to Mr. Michael Jackson—granting him complete, unrestricted custody.

When I asked around school, one boy said Mr. Jackson was known for taking in "lost souls." Quite a few kids stayed with him, and the students thought of him as a "good guy." But they stumbled when I asked them to explain why this sainted black man took in only white, blond, and young teen boys.

When a father beats a child to death with an aluminum baseball bat, it makes the headlines of the daily news. Officials reprimand the social service agencies and heads roll. But when someone chips away a child's life one disgusting trick at a time, there are no headlines. Slowly eating away at a young life simply does not make the sensational headlines the way bullets, bombs and bats do.

Four years later, "Mr. Jackson" was finally arrested under his real name for running a male prostitution ring. Even though the school and social welfare people knew about him, they did nothing to prevent the man from acquiring and selling white boys. Where was the father? What did the stepmother think a Michael Jackson look-a-like would want with a 13-year-old blue-eyed blond? Why did we pay such people to serve as guardians for our lost children? Why did everyone look the other way and tell me it was none of my business?

The story barely made the local and state section of our newspaper. I read the article in the paper word-for-word to my husband. I couldn't believe that I had actually met this horror of human flesh. My husband listened as I read it to him, and he shrugged.

Paying $20 for a Nickel Bag

"This was the most unkindest cut of all"
Julius Caesar

What kinds of kids are involved in the high school drug trade? The drug business ensnares all kinds of students, from all types of neighborhoods, participating as both sellers and buyers. Jose came to school every day. If he actually had paid attention, he would have been a model student. But Jose was not on the campus to learn "reading, writing, and arithmetic." He was there for pushn' illegal drugs to eager buyers, and everyone knew it. He just was never caught red-headed, so no one impeded his progress.

With no intentions of learning one single thing, Jose would become disruptive in class and encourage the others to do the same. One day, after becoming particularly fed up with him, I asked Jose to see me privately after class.

"What's the point, Jose?" I asked, "Why in the world are you here?"

In a talkative mood that day, Jose said, "I'm here because this is where my customers are, Mrs. Revell! Listen babe, as long as those stupid white kids from the suburbs keep givin' me twenty bucks for a nickel bag, I'm stayin' in school."

So in order stop the drug trading, the solution was simple—getting your kids to stop buying from the dealers. What a concept.

Preppies in Gangland

Drug dealers and users come in all shapes, sizes, IQ's, and colors. On my way back to my classroom after having been called out, I passed the boy's restroom. There in plain view were two preppie white boys buying and selling. Just as I approached, the one boy handed the other the goods and was putting away his drug money.

I stepped inside the common area to the right of the stalls. "All right you two, let's go to the office," I said with an air of authority.

"What! What did we do?" they gave the normal reply.

"Let's just tell it to them down in the office," I retorted officiously. Before I could finish, one boy pushed me down to the floor.

"No way, bitch," said the fine-looking young man, so well-dressed and articulate.

I then caught a glimpse of him throwing the weed in a toilet between himself and me. I lifted my leg to push him out and he ran. His buddy was long gone.

Through the entire ordeal, five to ten students congregated to see what was going on, but not one helped or ran for help. I gathered up my body and what little dignity I had left. Then I fished the stuff out of the toilet bowl, which fortunately was clean. Wrapped up in a brown paper towel, the junk looked like dried-up broccoli heads, much like the shreds in my refrigerator's vegetable bin.

Upon returning to my classroom, I continued to examine the weeds and was ready to pitch them. A little cheerleader walked up to me and said, "Mrs. Revell, what are you doing with marijuana in school?" Well, that confirmed it for me. Several others kids started to mill around and they also assured me that I held bona fide grass. Apparently, I was the only person in the room who thought marijuana looked like cigarette tobacco. I decided to dispose of the weed immediately.

"What on earth are you doing with that stuff?" was the initial reaction of my incredulous dean. He had two things to say to me; first, "Don't ever do that again—they could have killed you."; and second, "Can you identify them from the yearbook?" After looking over the pages for a few minutes, I had to admit, "Those white preppy boys all look alike to me." I never saw them again.

Throwing Money at the Problems

Schools receive funds to establish programs in the hopes of controlling school-based violence and drug dealing. I witnessed that the money was often squandered and might as well have been set on fire to heat the classrooms.

A few years back, I had a student who was smart, articulate, and often gracious. Ernest had just one major problem—anger control. But he was salvageable, and I wanted to see that he received some support so he would at least have a shot of leading a productive life outside of prison. When I heard about a three-day conference on violence to be held in conjunction with community leaders, school administrators, and young people, I found the person in charge at our school to see if Ernest could be included.

"Has he ever been in trouble here at school?" she asked.

"Of course. He has been suspended a couple of times for fighting, which is why I am recommending him for the conference. I think it might do him a world of good to get away from here and see the real world."

"Then, he can't go," she said without hesitation. "They only want nonviolent kids at their conference on violence."

"That's insane. These are the kids who need attention now—while they are young and can still find a way in life," I pleaded.

Then she explained what these conferences were really about. Politicians, administrators, and other officials liked seeing their pictures in the paper showing them doing something with all the government money entrusted to them to curb drugs and violence in the schools. So the first year they invited violent and potentially violent young people to a posh hotel. It was the kind of place important people generally liked to congregate, where they would look good in the pictures with a nice backdrop. This would be their opportunity to "get down" and "chill" with the young people of the school system.

Unfortunately, the violent students who were invited broke a few elevators, threw some plants off of balconies into lobbies, and told the politicians and big shots to go "blank" themselves. You know, the way they treat school buildings and teachers every day.

Community leaders did not really like the violence, especially in their faces. And they really did not care much for these violent kids, especially when their antics were so socially unacceptable and downright scary. However, they did love the posh hotels, ritzy lunches, and meetings at the taxpayer's expense. So they came up with a grand solution for the next year.

The second conference was much better for everyone concerned—except, of course, for the violent students and their teachers. The organizers kept the gathering at a ritzy hotel and school-based non-teachers still brought students to look "politically correct." However, for this second year and every year thereafter, the big shots invited only student leaders, including the student council president, club officers, and other respectable kids. These young people were so much easier to deal with. They stood still for the pictures and were respectable enough not to ask any embarrassing questions, unlike those nasty ones from the year before. Those misfits were better left in the classroom in the care of teachers who didn't really need posh surroundings.

The "plan," if anyone asked, was that the participating student leaders would return to their respective campuses well-equipped to solve the drug and violence problems. Perhaps they could "rap" with the guys causing the problems, explaining to them that it is not nice to throw plants from balconies. This camaraderie, along with few posters scattered around the campus where non-reading violent kids chill, were sure to reach Ernest and his buddies.

What a great solution! Rich people did not get their hotels messed up. Officials in charge appeared to be doing something with all the money they were given to stem the violence. Better still, they would never have to look a violent person in the eye or run the risk of being pushed around in a men's restroom. Teachers were so much better suited to deal with those messy details.

I wondered if the funds could have been spent on less elaborate surroundings—perhaps the YMCA—and for more counselors with resources to actually help the violent kids. With a few more security guards, maybe the young men with anger management problems could have actually attended the seminars. When they returned to their schools, at least they would have had some knowledge to work with to address their problems. Perhaps the politicians could have brought their lunches in a plain brown bag; then taxpayers would actually be footing the bill for something worthwhile.

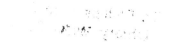

The Chinese Buffet

"Fair is Fowl and Fowl is Fair"
OOPS!
Macbeth's Witches

Sometimes a teacher says things in front of the class that she wishes she could take back—but of course, it's too late. And sometimes I was forced to follow through on a promise and was actually glad that I did. That was how I ended up at a Chinese buffet restaurant with ten of the nicest kids I ever had the pleasure to call my students.

Eddie mentioned that his parents owned a restaurant outside of town. This was after I mentioned that my husband and I were going to be visiting a local botanical garden for the fall moonlight festival.

"Why don't you stop and have your dinner with us, Mrs. Revell?' Eddie asked.

"Why don't you take all of us to dinner, Mrs. Revell?" Eric pushed it a little.

Thinking that teens would have something better to do with their Saturday evenings, I opened my big mouth and invited an entire class to the restaurant—sight unseen, menu unread, and my treat.

Ten students appeared, all boys who did not have anything better to do but drive out to have dinner with their English teacher.

Eddie was completely Americanized, but his Chinese family had little experience in the American ways. Our lunch party at least gave them a quick lesson on the American teenager.

We arrived and put a few tables together. The boys stuffed themselves at the buffet overflowing with chicken, beef, shrimp, and scrumptious vegetables.

After the feast, the boys became restless. They overtook the kitchen and even sang with the cook. We chose Mike to be the birthday boy. Then Eddie's petite mother left her cash register, Mr. Chow left his steaming kitchen, and Eddie's dad left his books to join a dozen Americans in a Chinese version of "Happy Birthday." They didn't have cake, so they passed out jelly-o's to all of the guests. In the mouth, they tasted like a Chinese gummy bear.

The time rolled around for us to leave and get on with the afternoon. We all spilled out into the parking lot, where Eric noticed animal pens with scattered food lying around.

Being naturally curious and not wanting the good time to end, we strolled by to the forbidden place, and observed roaming chickens, ducks, and one particularly large bird. These boys were city folk—they did not know what to make of the "big white thing" in the cage.

Eric took a look at it and announced to the group, "That is one big-ass chicken."

Eddie, being more fowl-aware, said, "That's not a 'big-ass chicken.' It's a turkey."

Children Playing
with Adult Toys

"To Be or not To Be"
Hamlet

Throughout the years as a high school teacher, I have observed far too many young people maneuver themselves into situations that they are simply too immature to handle. Most of these problems concerned their sex lives. During one school year, half of the young ladies in a particular class admitted in their writings to either being pregnant, giving birth to a stillborn baby, giving a child up for adoption, having a child at home, or having had an abortion. These girls were the ones who chose to share that information; the actual percentage may have been higher. The two presently-pregnant ones became so large that we needed special seating for them. They no longer would fit in the traditional "school girl" desk.

Not one of these girls coped well with her premature sexual experiences. I thought it odd that so many females were writhing in mental anguish over their predicaments, while not one of the male students ever considered himself to be a part of a parenthood problem. Were the girls getting pregnant alone? Did the father's horny situation become the mother's thorny situation? It certainly seemed so from my perspective. Never, not once in thirty years, did a boy express one drop of anguish. The girls were either suffering more, or were just more vocal about it.

The Girls

Wanted Dead or Alive

Kasey carried a soft satin photo album with her everywhere, even to class. Many high school girls liked pictures—of their day at the beach with friends, or at the prom or homecoming dance. But Kasey did not cherish something so typical. She treasured the images of her stillborn child in a full spectrum of poses. The photos included Kasey and the father holding the dead baby, the grandmother caressing the dead baby, and a group shot of the great-grandmother, the grandmother, Kasey, the father, and the dead baby. The dress was all satin and lace, fitting the baby perfectly. Perhaps the grandmother or great-grandmother of the dead baby sewed it especially for the occasion. I could only imagine that it was a tedious task to study for a test on the *Canterbury Tales* when you would rather be inspecting the photos of your dead baby. No one ever seemed to be sad—they smiled and posed just like they would with any other live baby. In Kasey's culture, this behavior was accepted and reinforced by all the attention she received from her peers. Thus, no one attempted to help Kasey modify her obsession with this lost child.

Thea's experience as a teen mother, although not as morbid, challenged her sanity all the same. She carried photos of her live baby that some other person cuddled, fed, put to bed, taught to pray, kissed, and who would someday accompany her when she shopped for her prom and wedding dresses. Thea opted for "open adoption" for her living doll. Thea often wrote and talked about her little girl. She delighted in showing her baby's pictures to everyone. The adopted mother sent photos so that Thea could see the child that she could not touch, talk with, or kiss. Of course, Thea's baby was alive, so the pictures had twinkling blue eyes instead of permanently-shut ones like Kasey's child. People grew tired of commenting on Thea's child day-after-day. A bit obsessed, Thea became a bore. So everyone began to avoid her and her picture book.

Joselyn and Carrie were not yet single mothers—they just had protruding bellies that could no longer fit in the traditional desks. We had to put tables along the wall with special chairs for our mothers-to-be. They poured over the photos of their classmates' pictures, probably wondering how their new babies would look (alive or dead). Neither ever spoke of the fathers or the necessity of a father in a baby's life. The only father who ever had a name was the one holding Kasey's dead baby, so he was pretty much off the hook. A year or so later, Joselyn checked me out of a local grocery store. As she scanned my food, I asked her how the baby was, and how she was doing in school. She gave me the same answer I heard from so many lost souls, "I'm starting community college in January." They all were going to begin right after the holidays.

Sandi

"That noise—it's a baby crying, I know it."

Sandi was only a high school freshman when she ran away with her older boyfriend, stole a car, got arrested, and became pregnant. When the boyfriend went to prison, Sandi went to the custody of her long-lost, baffled father. He had married and fathered a couple of pretty easy-to-handle kids. Then his daughter from a previous relationship was dropped in his lap. He tried earnestly—sympathizing with the teachers and taking her to the best professional help that money could buy—but to no avail.

I met Sandi ten minutes into a summer school class. She stood up, hushed everyone in the room, and whispered, "Did you hear that?"

"Hear what?" the puzzled class wanted to know.

"That," she demanded, "That noise—it's a baby crying, I know it. Someone has to go find her!"

The air was deadly silent. Sandi was removed from the class, and the rest of us finished the session uneventfully.

I saw Sandi again the next term when she was placed in a regular tenth grade English class. Since it looked as if I would be spending more time with her, I investigated her story. The assistant principal at the ninth grade center was not certain, but she was pretty sure that Sandi had suffered at least two abortions—one for sure. Now that she was hearing voices, Sandi was placed on birth control pills. Such troubled children suck a tremendous amount of energy from the schools and teachers. We were educators, not psychiatrists. Ultimately, they often dropped out of school, and their troubles spilled over into the streets.

My high school employed numerous guidance counselors, social workers, psychiatrists, and other helpers of children. Whenever Sandi and her beleaguered father needed a conference, many would implore Sandi, "What can we do to help?" They would even ask, "What can Mrs. Revell do to help?" After Sandi had cursed and threatened me, I no longer cared to change my entire lesson plan to accommodate her; I just wanted Sandi to behave.

The last conference I was ever forced to attend was led by a different sort of school worker, Ms. White, the tenth grade discipline dean. Instead of begging and pleading with Sandi to allow us to help her, or asking what the mean old teachers could do for her, she simply asked, "Do you want to come to school?"

No matter how the child twisted the words to suit her sympathy, Ms. White returned to the original question, "Do you want to come to school?" Sandi and her father were speechless for the first time. So many hours of conditioning from people who were "helping" led Sandi to believe that she was responsible for nothing. She expected everyone else to recognize her unaccountability. However, to Ms. White, she simply was unable to respond. No one had ever expected her to do anything before.

Sandi dropped out of school because it was no fun if she had to bear some responsibility. All the wrangling, almost a year of it, was for naught. A few years later, I found a note in my mailbox from Sandi. She finally had given birth to a baby and desired to meet me for lunch. I declined. I reserved my energy for the new ones I faced every day. Sandi demanded too much. Her problems went far beyond actually giving birth—she needed professionals on her side.

Camilla

Pro-choice, Poor Choices

Abortion stories did not always end with girls "hearing things." Camilla was a Hispanic girl with deep black eyes and gorgeous, long straight hair. She wanted to study hard and make something of herself. As a tenth grade student in my class, she was eager to learn. Open to new ideas, she was generally the type of pupil we teachers dreamed about. She moved on to her junior year with a close associate of mine. One day, Kathie sauntered into the teacher workroom and announced that Camilla was getting married.

"She's wearing a huge diamond rock. Camilla is telling everyone that she is pregnant, and that he is going to marry her," said Kathie, who sounded a little disappointed.

I too knew that it was a terrible mistake, but dismissed the entire tragedy. A month or so later, Kathie updated me on the situation. Kathie said she was shocked to learn that there was "no baby, no diamond ring, and no wedding." She was fairly certain that Camilla had bowed to family pressure and agreed to an abortion. Kathie seemed to think that Camilla was handling it well.

The next year, I had another turn with Camilla as a senior. On the first day of classes, she hugged me and expressed her glee at our reunion. While I remembered all Kathie had told to me, I never broached the subject of her pregnancy the year before. She did not mention it for quite a span.

Since Camilla had been in the same class with Kasey's dead baby, Thea's adoption story, and the two pregnant girls, she seemed less reticent to discuss her own circumstances. In focusing her writing, she seemed ambivalent about her young choice to terminate the pregnancy. She lingered after class a few days in a row, and then she finally sought out my opinion.

I did not give her the pat answer "It is your body, your choice" that I sometimes gave to be sure that I did not end up in the middle of family dispute. Rather, I told her the truth. I said that I wished that she were still a virgin still waiting to learn about that part of life. I wished she had not had to experience what she had experienced. I wished she did not have to deal with the guilt and the second guesses—the "what might have beens."

But, the reality was that she wasn't a virgin. She did experience an abortion and had to face the consequences. With all this as a given, however, I said that I felt she made the right decision for her life and time. After being exposed to these other methods of handling pregnancies, I was even more steadfast in my opinion. It worked for her, her life, and her future. Most important, it was done, and nothing or no one could undo it.

"Look to the grandness of the future you face. Love yourself for having the courage to handle adult situations, even as a child," I told Camilla.

She then seemed to put the matter to rest. In her writings, she no longer dwelled on her abortion. The future and her career became the focus of her attention. Eventually we never spoke of it.

Camilla modeled in a fashion show at a local mall, and I cheered her on. She called me for many years after her high school graduation, and I followed the progression of her career in fashion design. She still keeps in touch, but she has never married and has never mentioned another pregnancy. Camilla remains happy. She just needed someone impartial to the situation to tell her it was okay to be so.

Maureen

Dreads and Regrets

Maureen was born to a soldier and his wife. She raised herself and grew up so quickly physically and emotionally that she burned herself out prematurely. At age nine she began her menstrual periods, and at age eleven she became sexually active. A gorgeous blond with an alluring body, she attracted men from everywhere. Maureen's father was stationed in California when she and a seventeen-year-old beach boy got it on. Their union created a little girl that a twelve-year-old, even a precocious one, could not care for. So the soldier's mother decided to adopt the little one. The grandmother would raise her as her own and forget that mommy Maureen ever existed. Someone, somewhere, allowed a twelve-year old girl sign away all rights to her daughter. They told Maureen to go and start a new life and forget the entire incident.

Forgetting was tough on Maureen, so she would call once in a while to learn how the little one was doing. The grandmother became annoyed with the intrusion. So she changed her telephone number and forbade the father to respond to Maureen any longer.

When Maureen entered 10th grade English as a 15-year-old, she already had a 3-year-old daughter somewhere on the other side of the country. She was now a ravishing blond woman, compared to the others in the class. Maureen appeared so much more sophisticated, but deeply sad.

"I just want to talk to her once in a while," she would plead. "I won't steal her or do anything crazy. I want to hear her little voice, and maybe see a picture of her."

The main focus of Maureen's writing assignments was her daughter, centered around her self-loathing over giving her little one away and the eternal separation. How could a child know what she was doing in these circumstances? Maureen was surrounded by adults who just wanted it over. Having just gone through childbirth, she simply was too naïve to make such a monumental decision. So she signed the papers and now cried about it every day.

I would attempt to tell her that nothing is really forever, and that her little girl would be eighteen someday. Maybe then they would meet. Maureen would then tell her of the painful agony of the decision and the separation. Perhaps they could become friends. But fifteen years is a lifetime to the fifteen-year-old—Maureen just could not stand it any more.

Maureen's peers, while sympathetic, were clueless, and blissfully so. She needed professional help, or at very least, a support group. Lacking everything, she just did not want to live anymore. So, Maureen slashed her wrists in the girls' bathroom in the 200 Hall where all the English teachers live. I do not know who originally found her, as I was busy in my room with my sophomore English students. I heard Maureen was taken off to the hospital and that she would live, but would not be returning to school. I was not the least bit surprised. The saddest part was that the suicide attempt gave the grandmother even more ammunition against the child mother. It would now be even more difficult for Maureen to ever see her precious baby.

Maureen, if she is still with us, is way past being an 18-year-old. Her daughter would be a teenager. I hope for both of them that she has heeded my advice to get a lawyer—an excellent one—to review the contract signed by a twelve-year-old mother.

Tomeka

One Step Forward, Two Steps Back

Tomeka bounced into her sophomore English class tardy for the day and five days late for the course. She openly gnawed on her chewing gum and obnoxiously bantered with other students while she found a seat. The "glare" and "dare" were there. Many black students disliked having so many white middle-aged women for their English teachers. They "tried" them to force a response so they could figure out how to proceed with the entire year. They "dared" me to chide them, and they "glared" into my eyes to read my reaction. I learned to glare right back and dare them to try me again.

However Tomeka read me, she seemed to approve. She began coming to class regularly. My daily talk toned her down as I faced my challenges of her poor grammar and writing. Tomeka caught on well and displayed an interest in concepts and ideas she had never been exposed to. Other teachers noticed that she dared less and asked for more—she wanted to learn and be respected.

Towards the end of her sophomore year, Tomeka decided to go after her first job. She was more scared than I had ever seen her. She came to me after school and pleaded with me to help her with the upcoming interview.

"How does I act? What does I say? You can helps me. Please, Mrs. Revell," she implored me.

So we spent many hours together doing mock interviews—she asking the questions, me answering, and then me asking, she answering. We discussed her excessive cheap rings, necklaces, earrings, and what they were saying about her to her potential employer. We openly talked about her gum chewing, her loud, brash voice, and her saying whatever popped into her head.

Tomeka had positive traits, including her engaging smile, her willingness to learn, and her eagerness to discover what else was out there besides daytime television. She had potential and she needed to get this across to her employer.

The school, the teachers, and the guidance counselors were her only hope. "Family" for her consisted of an absentee mother, an abusive father, and an opportunistic white boyfriend. She landed that first job, and was she ever proud.

Tomeka's grades skyrocketed, and several colleges offered her scholarships. She was on her way to an interesting and rewarding life. But then one day, her senior English teacher informed me that Tomeka had dropped out of school. She was pregnant, and her ignorant white boyfriend wanted her to stay home. He wanted her to be there after he had finished putting roofs on houses and had had a few brews with his buddies.

I was crestfallen, and I ached for her. A couple of months later, I was coming out of the garden center at K Mart and I saw them. Lumbering along, Tomeka looked dead, all the sassiness gone. Looking dumber than two boxes of rocks, the boyfriend exhibited no tenderness toward her. After observing from afar for a few moments, I left. I would have rather seen her chewing her wad of gum like a cow and mouthing to every white middle-aged teacher in the school than have seen the pathetic quiet creature she had become. And I believe that she would like me to remember her as I first knew her and what she had become at her best. So we never spoke.

The Boys

"Does it matter that we had sex by accident?"

It becomes infinitely more difficult for me to discuss the boys' reactions to premature sexual experiences, because it did not seem to affect them the same way, if at all. When counseling young couples—who came to me for whatever reason—the comments from the boys seemed to be scarce and indifferent.

For example, when one sexually-active young man in my assigned group was asked what he would do if Debbie became pregnant, he magnanimously replied, "I'd do the right thing by her. I'd even take the day off from school to be with her when she delivers." This person is procreating out there somewhere.

Another young man murmured that Kaley's parents did not seem to care much for him, which might make the baby's life a little difficult. I looked at him, paused, and then watched his astonishment as I flatly informed him that not only did her parents not have to 'like" him, but that they could throw his white rear end into jail for performing statutory rape on their little underage girl. Here was a boy intelligent enough to be taking Advanced Placement Chemistry Class with my son, but no one ever mentioned to him that it was illegal to be sexually active with fifteen-year-old girls. Did we feel his "pain?"

His brilliant comeback was, "Does it matter that we had sex by accident? We never planned to do it."

Some boys reveled in bragging about their conquests. One youngster proudly ambled up to my desk to display the photograph of his newborn, his third child. Considering he was still a sophomore in high school, I pushed the picture aside.

"Don't you like babies, Mrs. Revell?" he asked, seeming genuinely disappointed.

"I love babies, Marcus. Especially the ones born to adults with the means to care for them, so I do not have to pay for them," I answered.

He chortled, looking from the class to me, as if he alone had the answer to a classroom question. Finally he announced, proud as punch, "You don't pay for my babies, Mrs. Revell. Medicaid does!" So I missed an opportunity to educate him about who "Medicaid" really was—I just couldn't carry on with him any longer.

The last boy was my favorite. He announced one day that he and his honor-student girlfriend were about to become parents. Paying the expenses, getting up at night, visiting the doctor were not fun, but he accepted them as his responsibility.

"Jack, I thought you had more sense than to get Courtney pregnant. Don't you know about birth control?" I asked.

"I know all about birth control, Mrs. Revell, but the rubber broke. I guess I was just too much for it," he explained proudly.

Happily, this father, mother and baby have stayed together in the relationship. Jack and Courtney finished college, and the little princess took right to my arms when daddy brought her on campus to visit his old English teacher. She loved her daddy.

Celebrities

"Everyone wants to grow up to be rich and famous.
Try for 'rich' and see if that doesn't do it for you."
Bill Murray

Joey Fatone of N'Sync was a classmate of my son's. Wayne Brady appeared as Judd in our school's production of "Oklahoma." He delighted my daughter and friend when he came from backstage to greet them and discuss his interpretation of the role. I, however, never taught any of the celebrities who passed through the school. Although she was on my class list, I never saw a Mouseketeer who claimed to be attending school—who knows if she ever received a diploma. The closest I came to teaching a celebrity were a model, Jay, and a Back Street Boy's girlfriend, Tiffany.

Jay and Tiffany were friends who were in the same senior English class with me. We huddled before class to discuss what the "Boys" were up to. My niece, Kara, loved to hear that I knew someone who knew one of the boys. She even said some years later, "I wish Tiffany had married A J, because then we could visit them all the time." Tiffany did not marry him, but I did enjoy her brief courtship, as I am certain she did.

"Mom, are you going to chaperone for Senior Night this year?" my daughter queried me over the telephone.

"I doubt it. Why would you care?"

"I don't, but two of my sorority sisters just have to go to see the Back Street Boys. They're crazy about them."

"Excuse me, but aren't they a bit too old for BSB?"

"I guess not. Anyway, can you get them in?"

"I'll ask."

After I did my best, the answer was still "no." Only high school seniors and their chaperones were allowed at Senior Night. The event coordinator, Janet, informed me that she would not need my services to oversee the graduates at the spring event.

When I informed my third period class that I was not going to attend Senior Night, Jay and Tiffany said, "That's too bad. We are going to be backstage and you and your entourage of Pi Phi's could join us." It's so easy to say what you would do—if you could do—especially when you will not have to do it. I let the invitation go, telling them, "Maybe some other time."

"Some other time" arrived the day of Senior Night, when two teachers backed out at the last minute. The head of the science department appeared in my room around noon.

"Janet is short on chaperones, and now she needs you to go to Senior Night," he sheepishly said, "Can she count on you?"

"Why didn't she come and ask me herself?"

"She's afraid that you'll be angry because she originally turned you down when you asked to help her out."

Remembering how important it seemed to these girls, I told him to give me a minute. After a quick call to my daughter, the girls decided to drive right down—final exams be damned. So I told Janet that I would chaperone, and I bragged to my daughter's friends, "I can get you girls backstage to meet the guys. I know some of their best friends."

That evening on a stage set in the front yard of a castle, the boys performed much to the joy of hundreds of screeching young girls. My husband and I stuck around to see for ourselves what all the commotion was about. There they were on stage, hopping over chairs, singing about undying love, and wearing silky white outfits and matching hats. The music seemed much like all the other boy groups, but the choreography moved with a fluidity that captured the attention of audience—especially the fluidity of the hips.

Between sets, I asked the security officer to go backstage to tell Jay and Tiffany that I was there. I knew that they would be waiting eagerly to take us to meet these singing and dancing boys.

"Nobody backstage has ever heard of Tiffany or Jay. Sorry," he added.

I reluctantly glanced around to see the girls completely crushed. How I wished I had not promised more than I could deliver.

"Sorry," was all I could muster.

The girls drove back to college after the show. I figured that I had heard the end of the singing boys. But the next Monday at school, both Jay and Tiffany fell all over themselves apologizing.

"They couldn't get us in the park—they couldn't even get their mothers in—and that's why we weren't there for you. Honestly, we do know them," both of them chimed in.

"Sure you do—whatever," I teased, "I don't really mind for me. It was Amanda and her sorority sisters who were so disappointed. That's all."

"We'll make it up to you; we promise. How about if we get them a personalized, autographed picture of the group?"

Thinking that it was just a waste of time, I gave Tiffany the names and the sorority of the girls. Doesn't everybody know a rock star?

The next week, Jay came to school with an autographed photo of the group, signed personally to me. He also handed me an autographed video. Tiffany brought an autographed photo for each of the Pi Phi's, and she promised that I would meet A J when he came to get her from school.

A week later, Tiffany dragged me to the parking lot curb. I wanted to tell her that it was okay—I really believed that she knew A J. As I was thinking about wanting to go back my room and grade papers, A J drove up in his fine blue Mercedes. Tiffany opened the passenger side door and pushed me in.

"Glad to meet you," was all I could initially muster, then adding, "Tiffany is a special girl to me. She and my daughter go back to brownies together. I'd hate to see her hurt by anybody." Impetuous but tolerant of my babblings, A J assured me that his intentions were somewhat honorable. I crawled out of his car, Tiffany jumped in, and I watched them drive away.

Later that week, Tiffany—who lived down the street from us—stopped by to say hello. Amanda had some friends over, and Tiffany volunteered to page A J to ask him to stop by and chill with us. At approximately 3:00 a.m. the next morning, A J responded to the page and called our house. Fortunately, I was fast asleep and never heard the phone ring. But my daughter was still awake and quickly answered.

"This is A J. Who's this?" he asked.

After a second or two, she found her wits and answered, "Amanda, but I think you're looking for Tiffany. She was here, but she left some hours ago."

"Oh, sorry it's so late. We were rehearsing," he contritely said.

"You can call here any time. Don't give it a second thought," she assured him.

"Yeah, well, right. Bye," he hung up.

As sleepy as she was, Amanda remembered him enough to tell me—and just about everyone else she has ever met—about the time A J called her.

Tiffany does not date him any more, and I've never seen him perform again. He was just a Back Street Boy, and I'm far too old to care about such things. But it did break up a teacher's routine, at least for a few minutes.

Jay has gone on to grace the covers of many of America's top magazines. I was proud to be his teacher when he was a lowly sophomore, and an arrogant senior. He was a good-looking, but modest young man; I miss his company and his generous spirit.

I still have the autographed picture Jay procured for me. I have to hang on it for dear life. My niece asked me once, "Aunt Mary, when you die can I have something?"

"Sure, kiddo. What would you like?"

"Your autographed picture of the Back Street Boys."

She'll have to wait—I have a ways to go.

Jocks Who Rock

"For let the gods so speed me, as I love
the name of honor more than I fear death"
Marc Antony

My school produced many professional athletes, and I had the privilege to teach a few. Dealing with coaches was infinitely easier than conferencing with parents, so I welcomed athletes with open arms. One call to the coach, and my problems with that particular student were over. I had no control on getting the athletes scheduled into my classes, but once they were there, I thoroughly enjoyed the situation. I attended all sorts of events, from the major sports to wrestling, volleyball, and softball. I still have all-state runner Dediere's Mickey Mouse blanket that she used to cover with in my room because she was always so cold. Buzzy signed a baseball for me which I will always cherish, because he did the right thing by growing up at Georgia Tech before turning pro. Many, many more dreamed of becoming professional football and basketball players. But after a stint in college, their dreams did not work out. They all had to find something else to do, using their brains—not their muscles.

The 1998-99 school year produced two of my favorite student athletes. Coincidentally, both had a real potential to make their livings playing games. As with many high school players, they focused much of their lives on the game, rather than the books. So when college time rolled around, the struggle began to meet NCAA requirements of the GPA, ACT, and SAT. They all repeated the common lament, "Why, oh why, didn't I pay more attention in school?" In desperation, they turned to the senior English teachers for any extra help they might offer—from writing skills and vocabulary to tutoring tips for the tests.

Jared and Terrence were friends with each other and with me. Their senior years in high school were so similar, it was scary. In the end, it was a miracle they both finished high school unscathed.

Jared

The Mercury Man Dodges a Bullet

Jared's reputation preceded him into the classroom—both his reputation for catching and running with footballs (as the "Mercury Man") and his reputation for giving the teachers trouble. I expected the worse, but was pleased with the best. It seems he was misunderstood on both counts. It turned out that Jared was called the "Mercury Man" because his father drove a big car to his little league football games—not for his swift feet. He admittedly gave his previous teachers fits whenever and however he could. But by his senior year, with the guidance of family and coaches, he decided to mature. Fortunately, I reaped the benefits of his change of attitude. Jared became my protector and defender.

In class, Jared became more attentive, eager, and cooperative because he knew he had to get his GPA up, pass the high school competency test, and score reasonably on the ACT. He was in a particularly large class with more than a few known rowdies—the males outnumbered the females two-to-one. I had to keep the lid on at all times. Whenever maintaining control became difficult, Jared would stand up and say, "Let her teach. You all be quiet now." And everyone listened to the "Mercury Man."

That year I attended every football game, not as a teacher obligation, but because of the heightened level of excitement knowing Jared might make the winning touchdown catch. Our team did well, making it farther than any previous team. Jared would come into class and describe a particular situation on the field—and we'd be all ears.

It was off the field that we almost lost our football coach, some key players, and Jared.

After having a spat with one of our football players, a girl sent her boyfriend to "teach him a lesson." Our boys were on the way to the football field for practice when the boyfriend and a fellow thug stopped the group in order to "beat up" a few of them. Clearly, these two criminals drew upon a high level of stupidity in their choice of whom to fight. Two old men of twenty-eight might have had a prayer with the girl's chess team, or even the drama club—but the varsity football team?

When it became obvious that they did not have a ghost of a chance, one thug decided to take the violence to the next level—he returned to his car to get a gun. Holding the weapon to the team captain's head, he threatened to kill him. The football coach arrived by this time, intervened, and pleaded for the boy's life. In the mayhem, the shooter fired several rounds, but his aim was off and no one was hit. Jared told the story to our class, how he jumped over some bushes just as a bullet whistled over his head. He admitted to being scared—some of the players even wet their pants—but no one was killed.

So, Jared became our miracle "Mercury Man" and seemed even more precious. As the year went on, it became clear that he was going to have difficulty meeting his dream of playing college ball. He needed a higher ACT score, and he needed a lot of help to get it. Several of his senior teachers were willing to put in that extra time to work with him. He kept trying, but he just couldn't quite make that magic number he needed to play his first year.

Jared's goal was to be recruited by one of the predominately black colleges and win the annual championship showdown. He promised me tickets for the bowl game where the two teams meet on the gridiron.

I couldn't resist the tease, "Will they let me in if I'm white?"

Jared replied, "Sure, Mrs. Revell. All the coaches are white. They'll let you watch."

Since most of the spectators were the alumni from the schools, I responded, "Well, it will just make it that much easier for you to find me in the stands. Look for a white woman."

After graduation, Jared was still trying to get his ACT score up where it needed to be. We met at a home accents shop that a friend of mine owned. Jared came into the store, attentive and polite. He was so helpful that he even opened a locked door on an Oldsmobile after someone left her keys inside. We went over to Wendy's when I got off work to go over some of the practice tests together. Jared mentioned that he had seen Skip, a boy from his class, a few days before. I had a smile on my face throughout as we laughed about the old times. And when we were through, Jared got up, promised to call, came over to hug me, waved goodbye, and walked out the door.

As I watched him walk to his car, without warning tears welled up in my eyes. I knew I'd see Jared again, I knew he would call, and I knew he'd be okay. But I knew most of all that it would never be the same. He wouldn't be there to protect me in class. I would not receive a Valentine's card from him next year. He wouldn't call me twice before my annual pre-prom party to tell me that he was trying to hurry along his date so they could make it to my house. He would grow up and find a life. And I would miss him.

I knew I would follow Jared's life because he was thoughtful enough to call and tell me that Terrance, his buddy and my student, had almost been killed in a terrible car wreck.

Terrence

Walking Tall

Whenever anyone complained that teachers did not work hard enough, or got too much vacation, I asked, "Do you want to be in a middle school at 2:45 p.m. the last day before Christmas vacation?"

Another question I asked was, "How about being the person in charge of an elementary school class on Valentine's Day, just before Easter vacation, or maybe Halloween?"

To me, the worst scenario was being a senior English teacher the last half-hour before the bell rings of the last class of the last day. The seniors explode. One year, the featured frenzy was water balloons, and I had a class of thirty-one wild people in a room with a sink and running water. One kid would cause a diversion on the side of the room, while another would try to get to the sink. Settling even the good kids down was almost impossible.

At last, the final bell rang and the mayhem began. Water balloons exploded all over campus. Administrators hurried the seniors off campus, so they decided to continue their battle at a local park. Unfortunately the skies opened early that morning with a terrible downpour, and they had to scatter.

Terrence scattered too quickly—while speeding over a rain soaked road, he hit a puddle with his SUV, skidded, and rolled over twice.

Jared sounded scared as he retold the story for me, "Terrence got out of the car and tried to act like nothing was wrong. But he just about passed out." Jared was in the car immediately following Terrence and he witnessed it all.

The car was totaled. Fortunately, Terrence and his passenger, Chris, were not. My future basketball player had survived. As Jared recounted the details of the wreck, I remembered the first day I met Terrence. At the time, I wondered if I would survive teaching him senior English.

Terrence's guidance counselor stopped me in the hallway to tell me that I was getting a new and interesting student. Already several weeks into classes, this was not good news.

"What period?" I asked her.

"Sixth, I think. I've had to change his schedule so many times that I'm afraid you will end up with him. You know—he's that basketball player's kid," she replied.

"Why is he coming here, now?" I asked, as if I could stop him or in any way influence the decision.

"Don't know. He was with Pete, but Pete's off sixth period. So now Terrance is yours, since you've got the lowest number of students in your class."

"Thanks," I replied, wanting to add, "I don't want him." But she was just doing her job.

Sixth period the next day, Terrence appeared. I'm a short person—I know that—but next to Terrence I felt like a miniature version of myself. At six feet, four inches tall, he filled a large space and naturally drew attention to himself. His classmates tried to be cool, but they couldn't help having a certain curiosity about this young man.

A teacher's main objective is to treat every student the same. They are like little piglets all trying for mother's favor. Whenever there was the slightest perception of favoritism, class morale unraveled.

Celebrities of any kind had the potential to upset my carefully-planned classroom atmosphere.

"Where shall I sit, Ma'am?" Terrance asked politely, while avoiding looking directly into my eyes.

"I suppose you'll need extra leg room, so let's put you right over there on the left hand side in the last seat on the first row," I pointed.

Terrence obediently found his seat and did not utter another word for a few weeks. He busied himself listening to the lessons and copying the homework assignments from the blackboard. I surmised the whole thing would be much ado about nothing. He would be no different from the hundreds of others who had sat in my senior English class.

Within a few days, guidance counselors were at my door again. This time Terrance needed to be moved to the third class period, same room, and same teacher. At this point, I was still oblivious to all the fuss being made about one tall boy.

When we held open house for the school early in the year, Terrence came along with his father, stepmother, and two little sisters. I remained calm and professional when speaking with his father—which was not easy since my eye level was his belt buckle. What made the greatest impact on me, though, was how pleased Terrence looked when I told his father how well his young man was doing in class. Terrence found his portfolio—albeit thin at this point—and beamed while his dad gave it a perfunctory look through. The other parents did not interfere with these fatherly duties in any way. But as soon as they all exited, a buzz came over the room.

"Do you know who that was?"

"My son is in the same class as Terrence."

"We'll be state champs for sure this year."

I ignored their comments and continued on with greeting the other normal parents.

Terrance was different; he could not help but be. The other kids treated him as special, so it was deemed okay for teachers to treat him as special too. No one ever forgot that Terrance was different, but he was so well-accepted because he never equated different with better. No matter what little girls came into the room to sit near him, or regardless of how the high school games went, he listened to all the comments and was polite.

When spring break rolled around, my nephew and a friend came to visit from Ohio. During their time with me, we visited all of the local attractions and went to a sports bar to watch the Pistons play. But when the time came for them to leave, I asked which part of their trip they would remember the most. Both answered without hesitation, "Meeting Terrence." Sure it was fun to meet a potential professional athlete, but it was more fun to meet Terrence—they liked him.

Terrence traveled to Iowa to participate in a national competition featuring the country's best high school players. He picked up a few mementos of this experience before returning home. Expecting nothing, I was astonished when he presented an autographed shirt for me and a personalized poster of all the players for my nephew, Daaron. That was the kind of person he was—even the biggest nerd in the class got attention from Terrence.

The day of the murders in the Colorado school, the class had a lively discussion about the senselessness and futility the crime, some of the causes, and possible solutions. We concluded that there were myriad causes and potential ways to prevent such tragedies. However, there was one item on the list of problems that resonated with the class—exclusion. After some serious talk about labeling and taunting, Terrence stood up, faced the class with his arms wide open, and half-jokingly said, "I love you all, man." Of course, there was some jest in the statement, but his classmates appreciated the message and applauded.

When the school year was almost over, Terrence asked me to go out to dinner with him. After some careful thought, I said, "You choose a couple of the kids around here to go with us. I will pick up the tab myself."

"All right," was all I heard.

For the next few days, Terrence would stop by my office frequently to ask if it would be okay to invite so-and-so and somebody-or-other to come. Each time I replied, "Whatever you think."

There were seventeen people in our party that next Monday night when we arrived for "All You Can Eat Wings." Luckily, the manager particularly liked Terrence, so he cut me a deal on the bill. Obviously, this was not what I had in mind when I said to invite a few friends. But as I looked over the group, I knew that they would never forget the time a teacher took them to dinner. And I would never have a better time in a restaurant.

My daughter, Amanda, was with us that night. As she and her friend went to the ladies room, a drunk followed them and commented on their looks. The overt flirting terrified them, so they ran back to me to ask what to do. I looked over at some of the guys and said, "There's a drunk over there bothering Amanda." Spontaneously, three of the biggest, meanest-looking guys leaped out of their seats to check it out. The drunk turned out to be harmless. But a chill ran up my spine when I realized what it meant to be connected when it counted.

Through Terrence, I achieved a better understanding of the pressures on these young boys. Girls were all over him. He was expected to justify everything that happened in the "big game" and remain cool about it. Most of all, because he was so huge, people equated his size with age and wisdom. They forgot that he was just a teenager, pretty much like any other teenager. What I enjoyed most was that great big smile and hearing every day, "What's up, Mrs. Rev?"

When prom time rolled around, just about every girl in the school would have liked to go with Terrence. He chose to ask a particularly cute and infinitely sweet young lady, Suzette.

One day about three weeks before prom, someone knocked lightly on my classroom door. The interruption was right in the middle of my class. Peeking thru the glass, I saw Terrence and Suzette—neither looked any too happy.

"So the reason you interrupt me is?" I asked impatiently.

Almost in tears, Suzette said, "Mrs. Revell, Terrence doesn't want to take me to prom anymore."

"You asked her, right?" I leered at Terrence.

"Yeah, I asked her, and I want to go with her. But I'm tired of everyone talking so much trash about it. I just want to go to the prom."

"Is this true, Suzette?"

"Yeah, but it's not my fault that everyone wants to be in our business."

Knowing I need to get back to my class, I said, "Once you ask, and she accepts, it is a done deal. You are taking her or staying home."

"Now Suzette," I looked at her, "You understand that this is a date, no more and no less. He is not committing to anything or anybody."

After she nodded, I brought their hands together, got a shake and a smile from them, and sent them on their way. I thought that there would be much more to this 'prom' thing, but was pleasantly surprised when that was the end of it. They went together, had a fabulous time, and are still close friends.

At the beginning of each school year, I told my students that I refuse to attend any more of their funerals—so they better take care of themselves. Terrence's wild ride on a wet road scared Jared and me to death. He promised he would never drive that way again, and I believed him. He has way too much to live for.

Duties Above and Beyond Teaching

"The fault, dear Brutus, lies not in the stars,
but in ourselves, that we are the underlings"
Cassius

I was allowed one free period per day to myself to plan classes, edit and grade papers, calculate grades, call parents, and perform other teacher duties. That "free" period must have driven the administrators crazy, so they came up with something else for teachers to do. On one particular Friday, I was sent to sit in the computer lab because the person hired to oversee the lab was meeting with another test administrator. No one knew why they couldn't meet in the computer lab while the students worked on the High School Competency Test questions. Or why they couldn't meet after the students had left for the day. But why would they bother, if they could force a teacher to come in the lab during her free period to do their jobs for them?

These students in the lab were not technically a "class." They were unable to pass a basic competency test needed to attain a high school diploma. So the school pulled them from various classrooms into a state-of-the-art lab for self-paced instruction. Administrators liked students to pass the standardized tests because it made their schools look good and qualified them to receive financial incentives.

Since the students were already identified as poor performers academically, a "substitute" situation meant nothing but trouble. Of course, any competent person would have sent them back to their normal classroom teachers when the assigned lab director could not be there. But on this Friday, they kept them in the lab and told me to go in to monitor them.

Things began poorly and moved to the impossible. Having absolutely no intentions of doing the slightest bit of work, several students began talking to each other and then decided to torment me. The chorus started.

"Mrs. Substitute, I can't figure this out."

"Hey, lady, what we supposed to do?"

"What you here for if you can't do nothin' for me?"

Now, in a normal classroom, these would be reasonable questions—but this was an exceptional situation. Each student was on a different program working at their own pace. They knew exactly what they were supposed to do; instead, they just wished to play.

One obnoxious kid was manageable, but when they bonded together, they were like a pack of wild dogs—and just as formidable. Considering they were not my primary responsibility, I decide to call in some help. But there was no way to get help, because I was stuck in a room with no call button or telephone. I would have contacted a hall monitor, but they had all called in sick (they preferred not to work on Fridays).

I finally decided to leave to get help at the office myself. Instead of sending the lab director who had made the decision have a teacher do his job, the office sent a sweet middle-aged lady. She had a heart of gold, but no disciplinary skills.

As she opened the classroom door, they all settled down immediately. Her only response to a teacher in distress was, "Looks like everything is okay now." She made sure that every student heard her. I was flabbergasted with her meek "reprimand." Not surprisingly, the worst-of-the-worst in the lab interpreted her response as a green light to raise hell.

I decided that if the office could not be bothered with this situation, then neither would I. So I read the newspaper as they laughed, threw things about, and wandered around. After completing the sports page,

I looked up at the teacher's instructions on the overhead projector. Her transparency had surreptitiously disappeared and been replaced with "This substitute is a psycho Bitch." At least they spelled the words correctly—they usually spell psycho as "sikeo." And why not harass the teacher? They already had already been told by an administrator that no one cared what they did.

I walked out. Another discipline dean handling another incident happened to be passing the room as I left. Handing him the transparency, I said, "This is what we're sent into. I'm not taking it anymore." Just then, the bell rang and one of the perpetrators walked out of the room. Unaware of the dean's presence, he said, "I don't have to worry—I printed all my shit."

The administration did not discipline any of the students because they decided that they could not really tell for sure who did what. And still they continued to send us into situations where there was no hope and no help.

It's Not My Fault

"Nowadays People know the Price of Everything
and the Value of Nothing"
Oscar Wilde

When American courts and Cuban exiles fought over a young child, Elian Gonzalez, I heard repeatedly about all the "things" he would have in America compared to the meager existence he would face back in Cuba. I wondered how all this materialism had affected American youth, and how it was translated into discipline in the schools.

Even with all the available state money, teachers still had to "float" from room to room as there were not enough classrooms to accommodate all of us. How many other professional people had to "relocate" every 57 minutes or experienced having another person using all of their belongings? Teachers did. Could a situation as the one I encountered with a rich young American have ever occurred in Havana, or is this attitude exclusively American?

All Too Precious Brat

"So since we are paying you, move your
ass in there and get to work."

One day as I returned to my room that another teacher was using for the hour, I stumbled on a young man arguing with his girlfriend. My exact words were, "Don't you have a class this period?" I recall my statement precisely—because students always did have a class and generally this simple question moved them along.

This particular young man, however, had not quite finished with his "woman." So he resented me when his girlfriend dashed off to her classroom. He then refused to budge.

He glared at me with such fervent hate, I almost feared him. All he could muster was, "Why don't you mind your own business, bitch?"

At this point, I was disinterested in pursuing any discipline because, after all, he was not my student. I just wanted to get back to grading English essays, so I would not have so many to take home that weekend. I reiterated my request that he find his assigned place.

His eyes narrowed on me and he lay down the final straw that forced me to act. His tirade started with, "My parents pay a lot of taxes that pay your salary. So since we're paying you, move your ass in there and get to work. We want our money's worth." Imagine hearing this in Cuba!

I could no longer ignore his belligerent attitude. Because I was helpless alone, I asked his name. He replied, "Donald Duck."

Fortunately, a stronger male teacher was walking by at that moment and was happy to assist me in escorting "Donald Duck" to the main office. After clearly writing up my report of the incident, I considered the issue to be dead. After all, he was not even one of mine.

But the issue came up on two other occasions. Once, when I was talking with a guidance clerk who happened to live near the boy and his family, she said, "The parents are filthy rich. They owned one of the original hotels downtown. They sold the business while they were still in their forties and retired to a lakefront home in a posh neighborhood. All they do now is hang out."

She then pointed out, "The mother is here all the time. The boy gives them nothing but trouble. He is suspended more than he is in school."

Although it should not have really mattered, I was almost relieved that I would not have to hear about him any more. What school, or parent for that matter, would hesitate to discipline a student with such an extensive record—who would speak that way to a teacher. Even in the liberal, open-minded United States, we still have rules, don't we?

Of course, I was mistaken that the issue was closed. A few weeks after the incident, the principal paid me a visit. He wanted to learn first-hand whether or not this young man truly uttered such words.

I could picture his mother in the principal's office accusing the school of "picking on" her "lively" son. After all, boys will be boys—teachers needed to understand and adapt. Besides, what did this nasty teacher do to provoke her baby? They felt their money allowed this privilege, and this attitude was never lost on the next generation. Why weren't these kids in private schools where their money might buy more influence? For a simple reason—many had already been expelled from all the best schools that money could buy.

My headmaster listened intently as I retold my version of the encounter. When I came to, "Get your ass back into the classroom," he said, "Stop, that's enough." His face saddened, he thanked me, and then walked away.

I never heard another word about that incident. So I assumed that the boy was reprimanded and suspended from school. No doubt, his parents continued "saving" him until this day. Alas, they had little else to do.

Jackie and Natalie

When a Brother Becomes a Sister

Jackie and Natalie—the names sounded like sisters and in some ways they were—except Jackie had been born male and Natalie female. Jackie remained a virgin throughout high school, even though plenty of females tried to attract his attention. In thirty years, only once did girls ask me not to seat them near a certain gentleman, because he made them so giddy they could not possibly concentrate. But Jackie had that effect on girls. What a looker and charmer! His dark curly hair tossed over his wide forehead just barely touched his coal-black eyes. He moved into the classroom with an assurance most 18-year-olds lack. Then one day he paled and seemed to lose his self-assurance.

"Can we talk in the back room after class?" he implored me.

"Sure," I replied.

After everyone left, he walked into the back office, sunk in a chair, buried his face, and sobbed. I could only guess that someone had died.

"My sister Natalie is no longer a virgin! Ninth grade and she has already had a sexual experience. Here I am a senior, and I've been saving myself. She's already ruined."

"Do your parents know?" I asked.

"Do they know? They're thinking of killing her! She left school with three other couples. She's not even dating this guy, and doesn't want to see him again. She was just curious about sex and what it would feel like. So they went to one of the homes and each went into a separate bedroom. They had sex all day long, until it was time to make the parents think they had gone to school."

"How did the parents find out?" I asked.

"When they were busted for skipping school, one of the girls spilled the whole story and named names. She identified Natalie as one of them, so our parents had to come down to school. When they finally all came home, I thought our father would kill her. He slapped her around a few times," Jackie explained.

"Slapped her around? Did you stop him?"

"I couldn't, but it didn't last very long. My mother cried and took Natalie to her OB-GYN specialist to be checked out for pregnancy—but the tests were negative. Then Natalie swore to both of them that she would never, ever, have sex again until she was married," he continued.

Jackie eventually settled down, and I consoled him as best I could. Mostly, I pointed out that he was her brother—not her father—and that all he could do was encourage her to take good care of herself.

Jackie graduated and went on with his life. The next year, I was surprised to see Natalie stroll into my twelfth grade class. She immediately wanted to know what her brother had told me about her. I professed total ignorance, and the year proceeded from there.

Natalie may have promised her parents she would never do "it" again, but she could not keep her promise—over and over and over again.

On a fine spring day, during lunch time, Natalie dragged in one boyfriend after another to meet me. She even attempted to make out in my back office, where she had cornered more than one young man.

Although quite promiscuous, Natalie never used any form of birth control. Her carelessness finally caught up to her. Cramping, bleeding, and bowing over in pain, she came to me for a pass to the office. I did not see her the rest of the day. Upon her return to school, she announced that she had had a miscarriage. The father was one of the many young men who she had paraded through my classroom as her beau.

So how did her parents respond to her miscarriage? Once again, they were deceived. The doctor who treated her was the same one who had examined her after the ninth grade tryst. While the mother waited outside, the doctor asked Natalie if she wanted her mother to know about the fetus. Of course, that was the last thing she wanted. So the man explained to the mother that some cysts in Natalie's uterus had burst, causing all the bleeding and pain.

Did the parents deserve to know the truth? Was it my place to tell them? If a medical doctor could lie straight-faced to parents, where was my obligation?

Her brother Jackie remained celibate throughout high school for a good reason. As Jackie matured and explored his own sexuality, he grew up to learn that he was gay. Thus, all the young women who he attracted posed little temptation. What he really desired were beautiful men. The parents took this revelation so hard that they refused to associate with their son. The mother was heartbroken, but she deferred to her husband's wishes. So they banished the boy from their home.

Jackie landed a great job at an island resort. Due to his parents' boycott, Jackie had no family members to invite to his show. So he arranged for Natalie, my daughter, and me to vacation at his island paradise.

Upon our arrival at the resort, I drove the big white van into a space for unloading our baggage. As each suitcase came out of the rear hatchback, the burly man said, "Does this one go?"

I would answer each time, "Yes, everything goes but the Laura Ashley bag. I'll carry that one myself."

Being caught immobile behind the wheel, I asked my daughter to jump out and grab the Laura Ashley bag so it did not accidentally get put with the others.

"Did you locate it yet?" I called to her, twisting to see what was transpiring behind my head.

"Mom, I can't find it—there's no Laura Ashley bag," she finally said.

"There has to be a Laura Ashley bag. It has all my makeup and shoes for the trip," I stated as if the more important the bag, the more likely it would magically appear.

"You left it at home. Face it," she finally said when the entire van was emptied.

So there I was, beginning a holiday barefooted with only my natural face. Fortunately, the girls shared their makeup with me, but I wore the same shoes for the remainder of the vacation.

As we entered the dining room for our first meal, we found ourselves seated with two couples who had never set foot out of Iowa. The tall man was a preacher who owned two suits, one purple and one green. They delighted in seeing Jackie on stage and then occasionally at our table. The couples couldn't take enough pictures of him with them.

A particular Asian waiter seemed to catch Natalie's eye in the island paradise. As we all sat around the table for our evening meal, she would stare blankly into the waiter's eyes and then provocatively run her tongue over her upper lips. Embarrassed by her callous flaunting, I implored her to cease—but she was determined to lick, roll, and suck. Finally the third night out, the waiter approached her and asked her to meet him after the dining room closed.

The rest of us went about our vacation business. Around midnight, Natalie found us. She was outraged, disheveled, and ranting.

"He tried to molest me in his room. I can't believe how bold he was!" she raved. "I'm reporting him to the resort director, and I'll have my brother see to it that he is fired."

It was senseless asking her the obvious questions, "What did you expect?" "Did you realize the messages you were sending?" or "Just exactly what did you have in mind when you went to a waiter's room?"

Jackie did the big-brother thing by approaching the confused waiter and flatly announcing that his sister was not a sex toy—even though he knew she was. Was it that she didn't want to be a tart and wanted protection from herself? No one was quite sure.

When Jackie heard the entire story, he shrugged, "I'm sure what you're saying is true, but she needs me to defend her, so I do." Jackie suffered from his own sexual identity mystery and was in no position to give advice to his sister.

When Natalie finally graduated from high school, both Jackie and I attended her graduation party. Some of the young people brought along swimsuits to enjoy the refreshing water on a hot summer afternoon. Natalie paraded around in front of her father, uncles, brother, and family friends in the skimpiest, most revealing suit ever created. I often mused why her mother never objected to Natalie's exhibitionism.

Jackie and I spent the afternoon together, as we were both misfits at the family party. He was finally getting his life together, and was quite proud of his accomplishments as a singer. He had found a partner who he hoped to settle down with. They had even talked of having Natalie carry a child for them when they were ready to start a family.

After extending my thank you's and goodbyes, Jackie's father followed me out to my car. I wondered if he was going to thank me for all the attention and guidance that I had given his children—much more than I bestowed upon merely average students. I had attended many of their plays, recitals, and even their professional performances. Instead, he confronted me while I was alone to blame me for his son's homosexuality.

"If you were not so accepting of his lifestyle, he would have to change," he said. "I have forbidden his mother to associate with him, and she listens to me. Then you have to screw it all up by being a kind of mother to him—one who accepts his deviant lifestyle."

Overwhelmed, I could barely utter a word to him. But I managed, "I'm sorry that you interpret my caring interest that way. Your children have always approached me; I did not approach them. They seemed to be looking for something that they could not find at home. And I guess I understand now what it is."

The father did not respond well. He insisted that I cease any relationship with his gay son, convinced that the boy would "convert" back to "normalcy" if he were forced to do so.

That was a new one for me. I thought I had been blamed for everything but the sinking of the Titanic, but now I was responsible for people's sexual orientation. Teachers must have enormously thick skin to survive.

Chelsea
No Good Deed Goes Unpunished

Even when we gave in to parental pressure, it somehow always ended up being our fault—never theirs. A few years ago, as I glanced through my new class roles, I recognized the name of a young lady who would be joining me that year. Because I knew her parents socially, I considered having her transferred to another teacher. But I didn't, and I paid dearly for this ambivalence.

As the school year progressed, Chelsea felt more and more of a compulsion to tell me how much she despised her father. She informed me that he was not her "real" father. Her pregnant mother had married Stan, who adopted Chelsea as soon as she was born. Until she mentioned these circumstances, I had not really noticed that Chelsea did not at all resemble her father or her half-brother. Chelsea was fair skinned and heavy set, while the others were dark and athletically built. Parents of adopted children tend to be protective and sometimes defensive about their children. So I didn't bring up the subject again.

The weeks rolled by. Just about every day Chelsea would tell me, "As soon as I turn 18, I'm leaving them and you won't see me in class again."

This statement was a common mantra of the spoiled children so I ignored it. Then one day I overheard another teacher say in our workroom, "You know that her father emotionally and psychologically abuses her. He forces her to stand naked in front of a mirror and admit that she is too fat."

I inquired, "So what is being done about it?"

"She is staying with a friend now, so she is safe. When she turns eighteen next week, she will leave the bastard for good."

The magic date arrived, and Chelsea disappeared from school. Her name was never uttered. I hoped that Chelsea had found some serenity in her life.

Soon it was March, and the seniors got antsy; they could smell graduation. An administrator came to my room to implore my help.

"I've got Chelsea's mother in my office and she wants to enroll her back in school. Any chance she can pass your English class? She cannot graduate without an English credit," he explained. He found it difficult to look me in the eye, as we both knew she should fail.

His question challenged my professional judgment. Chelsea had done nothing for three months; however, she was an A+ student before she left. What to do?

"Sure. If she jumps in immediately and gets her A grade back, then I can see an A and an F averaging to a C. That's what she needs to pass," I replied.

So Chelsea came back. Where had she been? She had left her parents for the welcoming arms of a boyfriend, who abandoned her immediately upon hearing of her pregnancy. She had told everyone she met how ecstatic she was to be carrying Anthony's baby. Unfortunately, he wasn't! So Chelsea aborted the fetus, crawled back to mommy and daddy, and returned to the classroom.

She never moaned much about parents after that. Chelsea did do A quality work, and thus, graduated with her class. So this should have been the end of the story. I would have forgotten the incident and probably never included it this book—but the saga continued.

Chelsea left high school, but within the year she found herself pregnant again. This time the father married her shortly after little Tommy was born. But they soon divorced and again she returned to her long-suffering parents.

Later that year, I happened to see her mother and asked her how Chelsea was doing.

"She is all screwed up and I know who is to blame!" was her unbelievable reply. I then expected to hear that Chelsea's problems were due to Anthony, her ex-husband, her adopted father, the half-brother, or the mother, herself, But the mother continued, "Those damn teachers at the high school! If they had not let her come back and graduate, she wouldn't be so messed up. The teachers should have forced her to redo her senior year—then she would have learned not to be so irresponsible!"

Right, Mom. Chelsea's problems were due entirely to the teachers—not the boyfriend, or the ex-husband, her abusive father, and certainly not the mother who stood by and watched it all happen. It must be the teachers' fault.

Katie

The Blame Game

Amazing as it was, not even Chelsea's story comes close to Katie's situation for displacement of blame. At least the teachers were acquainted with Chelsea. In Katie's case, her mother had compiled a lifetime of being self-centered and making just plain bad decisions. When her daughter began to exhibit the symptoms of "pathetic parenting," Mom blamed the most likely of persons—someone her daughter had never even met—her husband's ex-wife.

Mom had quit high school to get married just before she gave birth to stillborn twins. Once that marriage failed, she married again in her teen years. In this second marriage, she bore a son and a daughter. The son became her "favorite" so she doted on him at the expense of her daughter, Katie.

By her mid-twenties, Mom finally realized that there was little future in being married to a drug-addicted derelict, even if he was the father of her children. She had to support her family by working long factory hours and placing her children with indifferent childcare workers.

As Mom noticed that many women had much more that she had, she decided to do whatever it took to get out of her plight. The answer included the seduction and eventual marriage to her befuddled boss. Both he and she lost custody of their children; his went to their mother while hers went to the drug-addict father. But what did it matter, as long as Mom was no longer living in a double-wide on an alley.

Katie grew up to lack a work ethic and failed to graduate from high school. Predictably, she became a teen mother, a shop-lifter, and a drug addict—just like her father. After speaking with her "parents" on many occasions, I was stunned to learn where they lay the blame.

Mom bellowed, "My husband's ex-wife caused all of Katie's problems!"

I had to bite on her provocative statement, "Oh, how so?"

"Well, his ex-wife raised her own children to be such 'snobs.' Her children were high school honor students, and both became college graduates. Because my poor children could never feel comfortable around them, they developed low self-esteem. Obviously, this has caused all of their problems," she prattled on. "So you see," she continued, "it really is all her fault."

Julia

"Have a nice life—somewhere else."

Do we need yet another example of how money cannot buy happiness? Poor little rich girl, Julia, lost her father prematurely so mom found another rich man to marry. Unfortunately for Julia and her brother, however, the rich man despised having youngsters about. Children messed up his perfect rich life.

So the step-father sent the little brother off to boarding school and gave Julia a new Jaguar, her own apartment near the school, and plenty of birth control pills—everything needed for her to have a nice life.

With her life spiraling out of control, Julia clung even more to her boyfriend, Kurt. She sometimes coddled him, often chastised him in public, and cajoled him into submission. When the suffocation became too much for the teen boy, he attempted to break off relations with her.

Kurt's moves to untangle himself sent Julia to even more desperate measures. She resorted to what she had been taught by the significant adults in her life, "If you want it, buy it at any cost." So she offered Kurt cash payments to stay with her at least until the spring prom.

The boyfriend did not want to be purchased by Julia, but he became concerned for her welfare because of what might happen if she did not get her way. This all climaxed just before Christmas vacation, so I recommended that he break it off with her before the holidays. Then she could go home and forget all about him.

"She's not allowed in the house for Christmas," Kurt replied. "Her step-father will not hear of it. Instead, they are flying Julia and some of her closest friends to Europe on a private jet so she will not be alone."

Merry Christmas, Julia!

Non-Teachers

"This is a slight unmeritable man, Meet to be sent on Errands"
Marc Antony

Frank McCourt in his best seller, *Tis*, explains the motivations of guidance counselors and administrators. They used to be teachers and coaches who ran out of the classroom as soon as they could, each exclaiming—as taught in correspondence graduate classes— "I feel I am doing even more good and can touch more children's lives doing what I am doing now." That is, spending no time at all in the classroom where children actually learn something. I heard this boastful claim repeatedly from those who still wanted the status of "teacher" without having the stress of "teacher" work.

Teachers quit not because of the money, but because of being treated worse than the students—who can at least bring in a parent for a conference. First-year teachers were particularly vulnerable to "bored former coach" administrators who enjoyed bringing people to tears.

Waiting for Guidance

My first year, during an illustrious faculty meeting, we were asked to be "proactive" on campus, and not look the other way when we saw a problem. I actually believed that they were serious about teachers reporting concerns. So, when I witnessed myriad students jumping over fences and walls into the adjoining neighborhood, I said something to Mr. Ford, the man in charge. Being a resident of this particular neighborhood, I had heard the complaints of mothers who feared to let their preschoolers play in their own backyards because of these truant students appearing over the walls.

When I decided to "help," I had no idea what I was setting myself up for. After reporting the situation to Mr. Ford—thinking he would be interested in stopping the trespassing before the community initiated a formal complaint—I was surprised when he growled, "Why don't you just do your job and let me do mine." He did not even pretend to listen or care.

"I thought I was doing my job. Remember, we were asked to be proactive," I innocently replied.

His response, from a professionally-paid person about to be promoted to being a principal, was immediate, "You people come in here from up north and think you can tell us how to run things. Well, I don't need or want your help."

Stunned at the way he spoke to me, I ambled away, thinking I would never have to speak with him again if I could avoid it. But his harassment had only begun. He began belittling me at every turn and actually followed me around looking for ways to degrade me. Being new, I thought this was part of the initiation drill. Then one day he stepped so far out of bounds, I called him on it.

Mr. Ford appeared in my classroom first period and ordered me to his office. He gave me no instructions as to what it concerned or what to bring. All I heard was, "Come to 116 when this class is over," as he banged the door to Room 216 shut.

When I went as ordered to his office, Mr. Ford was not there. His staff informed me that he was across campus in another office. Not being sure what to do, I decided to pursue him to again ask what the meeting was about.

Mr. Ford simply refused to answer me, but he did order me to follow him back to his office. There I was—a professional woman—following Mr. Administrator without a word being spoken between us.

Upon arriving at his office, I immediately recognized a troublesome young lady from my first period class, Doris.

"Doris, tell me and Mrs. Revell why you cannot learn anything in your sophomore English class," were the first words that he spoke.

So Doris had her cue, and she was off. "Well, Mrs. Revell just expects me to know how to do a research paper. She never explains anything. She's mean and tells me to sit down all the time."

Finally, Mr. Ford decided that I was worthy of being addressed. He asked, "Mrs. Revell, do you know how to teach? And if so, why aren't you teaching this girl?"

My face became completely flushed. I should have left that very moment and reported to my principal what had just happened. But since they were old coaching buddies—and I was new—I decided to handle it myself.

"First of all, Mr. Ford, Doris has been absent over fifteen times this grading period alone. Today, if she had come in late again, it would have been her tenth tardy which would have meant a detention. I cannot be positive on the exact numbers, since you did not tell me to bring my record book. But I suspect that she was going to be late again—and rather than face the consequences—she found a sympathetic ear in here."

Looking to Doris, Mr. Ford asked, "Do you think these numbers might be close?"

"Maybe," she whispered, losing her punch.

So I asked her a few questions, "Have you ever come after school for help?"

"Are you continually late?" and "Do you ever make-up anything that you miss?" Of course, the answer to all of these was, "No."

"Do you shout at me in class and expect me to hold everyone else up while you lamely attempt to catch up?"

"Yes," she muttered as her responses got ever quieter while she stared at the floor.

Looking at Mr. Ford, I asked, "Am I supposed to usurp the times from the students who actually come to school, so Doris can figure out what's what?"

"Well, she never gave me the whole story," he stammered out.

"Go to your next class, Doris. I'll talk to you later," Mr. Ford directed as he ordered her out of the room.

She quickly scurried out. I believe that Mr. Ford expected me to do the same, but I wouldn't leave. I just sat there staring right into his despicable face. Finally, the awkward situation forced him to speak to me. Looking away instead of addressing me, he said, "Kids—you just don't know today." I remained silent and he became speechless. Eventually, I left Mr. Ford still fumbling around with his desk toys.

As I walked out, I considered three possibilities; one, talking to his buddy, the principal; two, seeking legal help; and three, going back to work and keeping meticulous notes for my book. I decided on the third option—to someday tell the taxpayers how their hard-earned money was being squandered on worthless administrators like Mr. Ford.

Have Gun, Will Travel

"Jorge promises to work to earn your respect again."

Effective teaching is a gift, talent, and a skill. Unfortunately, there are too many people paid to "support" teachers who do nothing more but cause grief to the people trying to do their jobs. Good teaching is more like good baseball. A great short stop for the Detroit Tigers said it best. He pointed out that anyone could stand out there in the grass of Tiger Stadium, get lucky, and actually make a catch. The talent—he aptly pointed out—was catching the ball day after day, week after week, year after year, and continuing to produce results at a Golden Glove level of performance. Those are the All Stars, just like the actual teachers who face students each and every day.

Teachers were assigned approximately 150 students to nurture, guide, advise, and—occasionally—even teach something new. We interacted with these youngsters for 180 days. Non-teachers and miscellaneous people had no regular, designated contact with the students, which gave them plenty of time to disrupt and badger the people who did.

My most glaring example of blind interference goes back a few years to a young man, Jorge. As a restless and disinterested student, he posed quite a challenge to teach in the 10th grade. His attendance was so erratic that I was not surprised to catch him out of class a few days before Christmas break. I drove across the street to a gas station to fill up for our long holiday drive. There was Jorge, lollygagging around with four or five other Hispanic boys in a vintage pink Cadillac.

Losing my mind for a moment, I asked him, "Jorge, what are you doing here on a school day?"

A string of expletives cascaded from his obscene mouth, as he made threats against the school. Then he told me how worthless I and the entire school were. At first I was embarrassed, but then scared.

Upon my return to school, I immediately reported the encounter to the appropriate administrator. His response was, "Good, I'm glad he's there, not here. I hope he means it when he says he'll never come back."

Unfortunately for me, Jorge did come back a few months later. He strolled right back into my sophomore English class. I asked him to leave and return to the guidance department—I would handle it later.

Moments later Jorge returned with his guidance counselor in tow. He told me that Jorge needed to stay put and that was the way it was going to be. After class, I explained to this Neanderthal the history that Jorge and I had and that I would not have him in class.

Mr. Guidance Counselor assured me, "Jorge promises to work to earn your respect again. You have to afford him that opportunity."

I found this statement particularly odd, because I never felt an ounce of respect for Jorge or his administrator mouthpiece.

The crowning insult came later in the week when another administrator—who was never involved in the situation until then—came to my classroom to reprimand me for daring to question the wisdom of a guidance counselor. When she heard the specifics of the case, she still defended his actions.

Several weeks later, administrator number one, to whom the gas station incident was first reported, appeared in my classroom, tapped Jorge on the shoulder, and said, "Come with me."

I never saw Jorge again. No guidance counselor, not administrator number one or two, or anyone else would tell me what happened to him. And, not surprisingly, not one of them could look me in the eye when I asked.

Finally, a secretary tipped me off that Jorge carried a gun to school—probably on a regular basis—and that he had been expelled for threatening to kill a fellow student. I felt confident that he was subsequently enrolled in someone else's county and someone else's sophomore English class. No one ever responded to my questions, and certainly never apologized for putting me directly in harm's way. Jorge could have easily killed me, and my family would have taken great comfort in the belief that he was "trying to earn my respect."

Why do so many teachers leave the schools? It is not the guns, or the knives, or the kids, or even the parents. It is the lack of support from above. The non-teachers keep hiring more of themselves to badger teachers, micromanage them, and then desert them when their support is needed the most.

Tragedies

"Beware the Ides of March"
The Soothsayer

On a gorgeous, sunny morning—and we had many of those—I stopped to consider how beautiful life was, and how fortunate we were to live one more day. That's what I was thinking about on the Monday morning after John F. Kennedy, Jr.'s plane went down in the Atlantic Ocean killing him, his wife, and sister-in-law. Who could not remember him as that handsome young man—the hunk? Again the family was immersed in tragedy, and again the world watched what was left of Camelot. Just about all of us were poorer and uglier, but somehow not so sorry to be us—alive to appreciate it all. The Kennedys did not have a monopoly on sorrow. At our high school, we felt our share of it.

One summer, a car full of our kids was speeding when it came upon a bus with its rear protruding into the intersection. With nowhere to swerve, the two vehicles collided at about 85 mph. Needless to say, they all died and four families grieved. Two of the mothers were teachers that I had worked with at one time or another. One cried all the time—at work, in the grocery store, and through church services. The other mother I never saw cry. She said, "I'm an English teacher. I understand tragedy through literature."

"Wow," I thought, "can literature do all that?"

The Brothers
Double the Grief

As a teacher, the worst tragedy I faced was the loss of prized young man named Peter and his brother, Stephen. Peter was tall and lanky and carried his musical instrument into English class with him every day. He loved to argue about any point. One day, we began to read "An Occurrence Owl Creek Bridge" by Ambrose Bierce. The short story is set in the American Civil War and it soon became painfully apparent that few of the sophomore honor students had any knowledge about that uniquely American tragedy. The first hint came in the story, as the men were identified as either wearing a blue or gray uniform—not as northerners or southerners. Not one of my students knew who was who. I asked them all to stop, get out a piece of paper, and write down approximately when they thought Americans fought the bloody war. The answers ranged from 1320 to 1956.

If it were a wise-aleck regular class, I would have thought that they were "playn'". But most tenth grade honor students did not play with mental challenges—they truly did not know. This was partially due to the contemporary concept that students need to focus on cause and effect, not dates. But the main result was that they simply did not think at all. How many Americans were there in 1320? How old were their parents in 1956? Did any of them bring back war stories from Gettysburg?

After I admonished them for such ridiculous responses, I encouraged them to think before they made fools of themselves again. Peter decided to challenge me. He felt that since they were in English class, I had no business asking history questions. He was a spunky guy who went for whatever he could make of things. I distinctly recall thinking that someday Peter would be someone's parent and would be embarrassed if his child wrote 1320 as the date commencing the American Civil War—whether it was in English, history, or art class.

The next summer, right after school was dismissed, Peter was killed along with his only sibling in a tragic automobile crash. No drugs, alcohol, speeding, or reckless driving were involved; only an immature response by an immature driver, who was uninjured himself. The driver over-corrected after running off the road, striking the oncoming car broadside. Peter and Stephen were instantly killed. As the news spread through the community, the grief spread with it.

At the funeral home, Peter and Stephen's parents were gracious. Having forced my reluctant daughter to go with me, I believed that we would slip in and out and barely be noticed. However, whenever there was a break in the reception line, his parents would come over to us and ask me for any quip of information that I might remember about Peter. I mentioned his always carrying his instrument, how tall he was compared with the other kids, and how interested he had been in the Civil War. They seemed to hang on every word. What I learned from this horrible incident was that every child in every class was important. It was part of my job see each one, know each one, and care for each one. I wish I could have had more for Peter's parents.

Many months after the funeral, my daughter was having dinner with a friend in a local restaurant when the parents strolled in. Even though she was only about half-finished with her food, Amanda left the restaurant. When she arrived home early, I asked why she returned so soon.

"Mom, Peter and Stephen's parents came into the restaurant," she said as if they were celebrities.

"So?' I asked.

"I thought if they looked at me, they would remember that I had been at the funeral home. Then they would be sad again and not able to eat. So I left before they recognized me."

"Honey," I hugged her, "they wouldn't remember you. And even if they did, trust me, they are hurting all the time now—nothing changes that. But I appreciate your thoughtfulness."

Every year, Peter and Stephen's parents took the money that they would have used for the boys' education and gave it to needy graduates for their college expenses. We all remembered Peter and Stephen, and how people who never met them benefited from their parents' enormous generosity.

Adam

Becoming the Man of the Family Too Soon

While the death of a son or daughter is the greatest tragedy a parent can face, it is still relatively rare compared to what many of my students dealt with—the loss of a parent. Most confronted their personal calamity with the help of family and friends; they survived and went on with their lives. Adam, however, had a grueling time coping with the sudden loss of his father.

Adam was in a small sixth period sophomore English honors class. He was the life of the party. All the kids knew him and liked his facile manner in every aspect of the course. In addition to his engaging personality, his achievements were exemplary. Then late in the spring, after a brief hospitalization, Adam's father unexpectedly passed away.

When we talked privately, I encouraged Adam to seek counseling for himself and the entire family, which now consisted of his mom and two sisters. He would laugh lightly and assure me that he would be okay. But his mom was going to a support group which he felt would help her. But Adam said he didn't need any help. After all, as his father lay dying, he instructed his son to become the man of the family and take care of the women who needed him.

A chill ran down my spine when I heard those words. My own father had heard them when he was only seven years old.

"Son," my grandfather whispered into the child's ear, "you are now the man of the family. Take care of your mother and sisters."

How does such a huge burden affect a child? In my own family, I observed that my father had his own methods to dull the pain. Dad found camaraderie with his fellow WWII veterans at the many social clubs he frequented. He would never miss a day of work. Nothing interfered with his taking care of the material needs of his loved ones. The words of his father never left his consciousness.

In Adam, I did not observe the results of his burden until the next school year. When he crept through my classroom door in September, Adam weighed twenty to thirty pounds less than he had in the spring—and he was not a heavy young man to begin with. No normal circumstance could have caused a sixteen-year-old to lose that much weight. Something was drastically awry.

"So is everything still just fine for you, Adam?" I asked after a big hug around his skeleton.

"Sure, I had a great summer. I stopped by to say hello, and wish good luck to this year's kids," he answered.

"Do you need someone to talk to? How about the counselors, the SAFE support team, or someone else?"

"No, I'm great," were the last words that I heard from him for a couple of months.

Adam was not fine. He desperately needed help, but was determined to hide his need. The final cry for help that got everyone's attention came one night when Adam and a friend were fooling around with his late father's pistol. Some depressed people play with guns as they contemplate using them on themselves. Although the ending of the scenario might have been tragic, it was really more senseless. Adam ultimately did not turn the gun on himself, but accidentally shot his friend in the arm. If he were looking to kill someone, he probably would have, but instead he inflicted a fairly minor, completely fixable wound.

Garnering attention was Adam's real aim—he finally got all he wanted and then some. His friend was rushed to the hospital, where he was put back together again, and went on with his life. Adam was immediately thrown into therapy. He seemed to be making progress, until the injured boy's parents apparently watched too many television commercials that began with "Have you been injured in an accident?"

Knowing that Adam's mother had received life insurance benefits and had some equity in their home, the lawyers would not settle for the $100,000 that the homeowner's insurance was willing to pay. They wanted it all—the insurance, the home, all of it. The lawsuit sent Adam back to losing weight and handling of knives, since all the guns had been properly disposed of. Guilt from the father's death, guilt for not being man enough, and finally guilt for the financial ruin of the family were more than a teenager could handle. Adam did not want to live any more.

Contrary to what most people believe, the quote is not, "Money is the root of all evil." The actual biblical account is, "The love of money is the root of all evil." More important, which is also grammatically correct, is what people are willing to do to accumulate the money they so love.

I often talked Adam through what he and his psychiatrist were discussing. My thoughts drifted to his mother. Here she was, the housewife mother of three children who unexpectedly lost her husband. She probably took some solace in the financial security she might have from the insurance policy. Then her son, playing with a gun, shot another boy, and the family with their attorney wanted everything she owned.

By the end of his senior year, Adam found some peace and got back on track. Although his mother worried, the parents of the injured boy eventually settled for the money from the insurance company. Adam put on weight, started dating a good girl, and worked to get his grades back where they belonged. I finally stopped begging him to promise me that he would not take his own life—I knew he wouldn't. When I asked how his mother was doing, he said, "Great. My sister is pregnant, which takes all the bad-boy heat off of me, It gives mom something to look forward to."

A few years later I received Adam's graduation from college announcement. I knew he had recovered, but what a cost to everyone!

Elaine

A Teacher to the Last

Students were not alone in facing tragedy. Although we rarely shared our grief with the student body, teachers certainly shouldered their burdens. When a beloved faculty member died, we were all at a loss.

My friend Elaine lost her husband to the AIDS virus, and then two years later, she died. She and I shared a room the first year she came to teach with us at the high school. As a fellow English teacher, we shared a love of literature and life. Elaine and Ted were never able to have children, so she made her students like her very own. In her will, she left me a Lennox vase and her collection of "I Love Lucy" shows on videotape. Every once in a while, when I watch an old scheme of Lucy and Ethel's, where they are mistakenly identified as "Pick-pocket Pearl" and "Sticky Fingers Sal," I remember my friend, Elaine.

Just before Ted died, he and Elaine celebrated their 12th wedding anniversary. At this last stage in his life, Ted was only mobile with the aid of his walker. When he wished to communicate, he wrote on a small chalkboard because he had lost his voice. None of this dampened their joy or the extent of the feast they presented to their guests.

Some faculty members were there in deference to their colleague, Elaine. However, they were terribly uncomfortable being around Ted and his affliction that permeated the atmosphere. Someone finally commented on how delicious the potato salad tasted. Ted feebly lifted his board and judiciously wrote, "Thank you. I made it myself."

One plump teacher had a spoonful ready to devour when she glanced over at the board. She slowly lowered her utensil from her mouth and pushed the plate away. A few minutes later, she and her husband left the party.

After another two years, Elaine displayed the ravages of the insidious disease. She continued to entertain, and her last party was a 4th of July pool party. She feebly lowered her emaciated body into the Jacuzzi, lightly splashed at the water, and looked around at her guests.

"Come on in and join me," she managed to say.

No one, not a single person, not even her brother or sister would go near her, so I did. I had faith that what experts were telling me was true, that the virus could not be contracted through casual contact, including potato salad and Jacuzzis. Sitting with her in the steamy water is one of my favorite images of us together, but not my last.

Elaine was such a "fighter." She taught school until the day before she perished—she gave her all to those kids. Since Ted's passing, she and I attended every spring prom together. That year, as I drove up to the handicapped spot, the doorman took one look at her and could immediately tell how weak she was.

"Will you be wanting a wheelchair, young lady?" he asked in a cheerful manner.

Elaine declined, walked in unassisted, and even danced. I remember how she mentioned that the music was a little too loud—the only complaint she made. Nine days later, she left school early, went home, lay down on the same bed where Ted died, and breathed her last.

Marilyn

Cancer and the Beauty Queen

Elaine was a part of my life for a few years—and the loss is still there—but another lady, Marilyn, was my dear friend from the time I arrived in my new locale until we lost her to cancer, thirteen years later. We met while working for an insurance company as trainers for their software packages. Fewer things in life are more boring than credits and debits, but with Marilyn around, they seemed almost fun.

Marilyn was one of the most beautiful, charming, and engaging people I have ever known. She had only one character flaw; she kept marrying men she did not love for a variety of reasons. The last one she married on February 14, 1987, the exact day that I married my dear husband. While everyone thought we were working on strategies for increasing efficiency in the training department, we were in fact planning these double weddings.

While Marilyn wanted her reluctant man to make the commitment, I was fending off my man who was all too committed. Marilyn had been divorced for many years, and Kirk had just lost his wife. I, on the other hand, was newly divorced while Charles had been single for over a decade. I concocted the idea of telling Charles that I thought Valentine weddings were the most romantic. This held him off for months, while I thought it over. So Marilyn told Kirk the same thing—that Valentine's Day weddings were the best—so she was able to get a calendar in front of him and set the date. One problem we hadn't considered was that we would not be able to attend each other's weddings. But at least, we would both got what we wanted.

Shortly after we married our respective spouses, we both quit the insurance business. I saw Marilyn occasionally at showers and weddings that brought the old gang together, but we were not close. I even ran into her at the grocery store were we both shopped, but we did not see each other socially. Then one day as I was leaving campus, there was Marilyn—as radiant and beautiful as ever.

"So, what are you doing here? I thought that your daughter graduated years ago," I asked.

"I work here now. I'm the new business teacher," she said energetically.

"What does Kirk say about you working? Isn't he embarrassed in front of his country club friends to admit that his wife has to work?" I asked, thinking that maybe she was working to keep herself busy or to feel useful.

"That cheap bastard never gives me a cent. I had to work to put Susan through college. I'm here because I have to work if I want any spending money. He gives me a place to live and a car to drive, but other than that, I'm on my own."

"I'm sorry to hear that, but glad you're here. This is going to be great."

When Marilyn joined the business faculty, I volunteered to be the Business Academy senior English teacher. That enabled me to work more closely with the business people, especially Marilyn.

So the clock had been turned back ten years. There we were together again, this time happier at the job. I was also happier in my marriage; unfortunately, Marilyn was not, but that did not stop her. Whenever she could, she participated in school functions, parties, and even ran Future Business Leaders of America.

With Marilyn leading the Business Academy teachers, the typical school day began at 7:05 a.m. in her room. We laughed, planned, discussed the kids we held in common, and promised to meet at lunch. Those were the happiest times I experienced with a school staff. Then more and more, Marilyn had to go home for lunch "just to lie down." Panic did not set in at first, as we all thought it was a virus that would soon pass. After the doctor told Marilyn that she had a terrible case of indigestion, she walked around with a bottle of Maalox in her hand, chugging as needed. The upper GI test was next, but the results were inconclusive. Something there was not quite right, so the doctors ordered a MRI. Even though swallowing became more and more difficult for Marilyn, we all thought it was nothing. Then came the official diagnosis—cancer of the esophagus and stomach.

As we stood in the deserted hallway after school, she peered through those clear, radiant blue eyes, and said, "Now, I have to face this."

"Marilyn," I said, "we've faced insurance software, hurricanes, bad marriages, kids in college, and now illness. Somehow we'll get through it."

"Sure," was all she said, but she did not look me in the eye. I knew then that this was the end.

Marilyn's birthday is November 22, and mine is November 21. Coincidentally, one of the other Business Academy teachers was expecting right around those dates. We were both rooting for each of our dates. Marilyn won, when Austin was born November 22, 1997, right on her birthday. On the day of the big birthday bash, Stephen, Marilyn's little brother, threw the biggest and battiest birthday party on her 57th birthday at the nicest, swankiest club in town. For our gifts, we were asked to bring one good joke and our best story about Marilyn.

If prayers, well wishes, and just plain love could keep someone from dying, Marilyn would still be here with us. But they can't and she isn't. She lived six more months and then died quietly in her home on a beautiful Saturday morning. Her funeral was almost as beautiful as she, and the tears flowed from family, friends, faculty, with by far the most from her students who adored her.

Violence

===

"Villains, You did not so, when your vile daggers hacked one another"
Marc Antony

If you watched your brother bleed to death after a drive-by shooting, how many days would you miss school or work? How many days would you be so debilitated that you could not function? How about none?

James

Murder He Wrote

James' brother was killed—shot dead in the street—right where James could watch him bleed to death. The newspaper picked up on the story, but I did not read it. The next day as class began, there was James sitting quietly in his seat. He was not even going to mention his tragedy. Another girl, who "stayed" near him, did.

After asking him if it were true and hearing him say, "Yes," (no more, no less) I decided to watch him closely over the next several weeks. The astounding part of the observation was this—no change. James interacted well with his classmates; he participated as he always had. The unfathomable truth was that he was not all shook up. He was not covering the grief that most people would feel and perhaps suppress. In his world, murder was a common occurrence—even the murder of a brother. James simply accepted the situation, went on with his life, did his homework, and gleaned what he could from his other world of school.

James was not alone in this world so jaded by violence it almost went unnoticed.

Youreka

"The one stabbed to death was my auntie."

In sixth period, Room 211, a shy, soft-spoken black girl liked to sit as close to my desk as possible. She would beg not to be moved further away from the teacher.

Sometimes I struggled with names and hers, Youreka, perplexed me. She sensed my confusion so she spoke up, albeit softly,

"My name is Your E Ka. You know, like the vacuum cleaner."

"Of course," I replied.

Youreka wanted to clean the boards or pick up books—anything—so she would not have to leave too soon. I enjoyed her company, so we would sometimes talk usually about school topics. I knew nothing of her home life.

After the Christmas holidays, she ran in early to class.

"You see the papers, Mrs. Revell?"

"Which one, dear?"

"The one about the stabbing?" she replied.

"Sure, did you know them?" I asked, praying she was just making small talk since we'd been apart so long.

"The one stabbed to death was my auntie. She stays with me."

After I expressed my heartfelt sympathy, I asked if her mother was doing all right with such a shock and loss. It was usually safe to assume "auntie" meant some sort of relative from the mother's side of the family, since fathers were so rare in her world.

"Oh, I never seen my mother. She's in jail, I think," she innocently replied.

So we had a child with a missing mother, no father, and a murdered mother substitute. Why had "auntie" been so violently attacked and murdered? At a New Year's Eve party, two women argued over a boyfriend. Within minutes, Youreka's twenty-nine year old primary caregiver lay in a pool of blood over a "boyfriend."

So I hugged her, and she hugged back. But nothing outwardly changed—Youreka just took it and often said, "It be's that way."

Shawanna

"She don't mess with me no mo'."

My first year at high school, I taught William Shakespeare's "Julius Caesar," which I had not read myself since I was a sophomore at my high school in Toledo, Ohio. I better understood what the master writer had in mind after Shawanna interpreted it for me.

Before Shawanna, my favorite quote as a teacher was Marc Antony's, "When Caesar says, 'do this,' it is performed."

I would recite it with my right arm extended and say, "When Mrs. Revell says 'do this,' it is performed." Right!

Through most of the classroom reading of "Julius Caesar," the sophomores barely paid attention. However, in the third act—when a mortally wounded Caesar looks into the eyes of his beloved friend, Brutus, who has not yet committed to the dirty deed, and whispers, "Et Tu Brute?"—a quiet sense of horror falls on the room.

Later in Act IV Marc Antony chides Brutus with, "When your vile daggers hacked one another in the sides of Caesar, you showed your teeth like apes."

I would then say, "Of course, none of us personally knows how it feels to 'hack one another'." Peering across the room, I spotted Shawanna with her raised hand. Thinking she would agree with me that "hacking" was inappropriate behavior for civilized human beings, I called upon her.

"I stabbed Sharika two years ago in the park," she unabashedly shouted.

"Oh," I managed. I was literally speechless.

"She was nasty and kept talkin' 'bout my boyfriend. So, I took a kitchen knife from momma and shoved it right in her," she offered on her own.

Attempting to regain control, but still curious, I asked foolishly, "Why are you still here in public school after doing this?"

"They don't do nothin' but put you in juvenile hall for a couple of months. Then I'm right back here, cause she didn't die," she explained.

Again dipping into my teacher reserve think tank, I replied in a scholarly tone, "Of course, class, we all understand that violence only begets more violence and nothing is solved or accomplished."

Before I could pontificate with one more word, Shawanna spurted out, "She don't mess with me no mo'." Subject closed, class dismissed.

The Last Word

Discipline Without Violence

From the detailed accounts of being beaten with objects including boat oars and vacuum cleaners, to a girl's story of her shock when her stepbrother crept into her bedroom with full intentions of raping her, tragedies are endlessly written.

Violence—the kind that makes one person want to inflict pain on another—saturated their lives. After reading *A Patch of Blue*, a novel assigned to the slower readers in the tenth grade, the class discussion centered on the violence the girl's mother imposed on her whenever the mother decided the daughter needed it. Many students expressed disapproval of the mother's actions because the girl clearly did not deserve it. However—almost without exception—they accepted, even promoted violence when someone did deserve it.

Simone's boyfriend slapped her around, but only, "When I am really asking for it," she assured me.

Anna vociferously defended her father's beatings with, "I deserved them and they made me a better person. It is how I learned right from wrong." Confused and equating violence with discipline, they planed to do the same when they have children. That is, teaching them right from wrong by inflicting a great deal of pain on them when they are wrong.

After one particularly loud argument, where some students were quiet and some disagreed with the majority, no one dared to agree aloud with my nonviolent philosophy. The class scurried out the door when the bell rang. One girl who had been silent throughout the bantering came up to my desk. She asked me to please tell her the truth. I swore to tell her the absolute truth about whatever was troubling her.

"During class you said that you never, ever beat your children and you that you never laid a hand on your daughter in anger. Is that true?" she asked.

"Yes, and Susan, that is the truth," I promised her.

Tears welled up in her eyes as she explained that she felt my children must be "perfect" because her mom only slapped her face swollen when she was real bad. How could my children be so good that they avoided needing to be punched until their eyes were swollen shut?

"Did they ever be bad?" she wanted to know.

I paused, holding back my own tears. Then I explained that many of our students were slapped and had their hair pulled out at the roots—I knew how much it must have hurt. No, my children had not been real bad. They were not perfect, but I swore that there had to be a way to discipline them without physical pain and humiliation.

So when I became a teacher and a mom, I practiced what I preached and disciplined without violence. Whenever the issue of paddling in the schools arose, I opposed it. At home, we discovered myriad ways to correct inappropriate behavior—all the physically painless way. I hoped that my students and my grandchildren would all benefit from this philosophy of discipline.

"They were bad, Susan—sometimes plenty bad. There were times I did not know what I would do with them, but I found other ways to deal with it," I answered. Then I assured her that she was not "bad" and I hoped that she would be able to find other ways to get her kids to do the right thing without punching them.

Twins

"Double, Double, Toil and Trouble"
Macbeth's Witches

As a young wife, I remember thinking that I might want to give birth to twins—with the crazy idea that then I would only have to endure one pregnancy to have a complete family. If raising twins is as strenuous at home as teaching them in the classroom was, I'm glad that I was never granted my wish.

Identical twins in the same classroom could be confusing. I still am not sure which one was Amy and which one was Joni; the same held true with Evan and Aaron. But even when they did not look precisely alike, they had their special needs.

Greg was in my second period class, while Brad attended the third and fourth period block. Having a common last name, and not being identical, it took me weeks to learn that they were brothers born at the same time. Because their mother was a teacher, she saw to it that the boys were well-mannered, well-behaved, and well-studied. So they were never a problem to the teachers. But I sensed a problem between them.

Brad was smarter, a better athlete, and maybe even a tad better looking than Greg. The boys' report cards provided indisputable evidence of Brad's superior academic skills. Sometimes, Greg would further translate that mom and dad preferred Brad because he was more gifted by God.

So, when I chose a short story to read and discuss in class, Greg blurted it out, "I believe that my Mom loves Brad more than she loves me." I knew Brad and Greg's mom and that it wasn't true, but I had no way of conveying that information to Greg at the time.

The story concerned a successful black man with a Ph.D. returning to his hometown in rural Alabama. He brought his son to meet the grandmother and all the brothers, sisters, cousins, aunt, uncles, and various sundry relatives. The Ph.D. resented his mother for what he saw as her favoring his brother all those years. After all, he had the doctorate degree and lived in sophisticated New York City. He was the most competent, so why wasn't he loved the most? This acrimony has been eating on him for decades. At the big family dinner, as the boy, father, and grandmother were bonding, the infamous brother strolled on in. He was late, dressed like a pimp, and talking some trash.

The tardy arrival of the wayward brother was more than the boy's father could stand. He started berating his brother, crying all the while. The mother of the two grown men was an uneducated, simple woman, but she perceived what was going with her two sons. In her own way, she tried to explain that the pimp brother had always received more attention than the smart one because he always needed more attention. She did not want any of her children to end up in jail or dead, so she did what she had to do. All through it, however, she assured her sons that she had loved them both and was so proud of them. This explanation did appease the Ph.D. and he ran up the stairs crying. The story ended with the question unresolved. Did the mother do the right thing by paying so much attention to the one child over the other?

Greg read the story with an intensity that I had never seen in him. When I opened the issue for class discussion, he was among the first who wanted to contribute.

"I was in intensive care for days, and mom never left my side," Greg remembered. "She was there because I needed her to be there, so I guess she loves me too."

It was like the old light bulb came on over his head, revealing the answer to his dilemma. Brad and Greg both needed their mom at different places, at different times, and in various ways. Brad did not question his mother staying at the hospital when the other boy needed her. And it seemed that Greg would no longer question his mother being at the basketball court or wherever Brad needed her. In fact, Greg was seen more around the basketball court himself. Both he and mom could root for brother Brad. He needed them to be there.

As their teacher, I relished the satisfaction of having something we read, that I chose, strike such a personal cord with a young man. Perhaps the lesson made some lives a little better to live.

Wild About Wilde

"Nothing Worth Knowing Can Be Taught in Schools"
Oscar Wilde

Oscar Wilde lived in the late 19th century. Although British, he loved America and Americans, and especially enjoyed traveling throughout the American west. Some consider him to be the second best English writer of all, directly behind William Shakespeare. His portfolio included poetry, plays, novels, and children's stories.

When our community decided to dedicate a year of theatre to Oscar—dubbing it "Wild about Wilde"—my English IV honors class delved right in. After reading *The Picture of Dorian Gray*, we met at the civic theatre to enjoy "Gross Indecency," a retrospective look at his life, time, and works. Later in the year we also read *The Importance of Being Ernest*. And finally, I attended a theatre presentation of "Salome," his serious study of John the Baptist's beheading. Fortunately, no other students were present when an alumnus completely disrobed in the dance of the seven veils.

Some of the straight guys from the class objected to focusing on Wilde and his obvious reflections on homosexuality that peppered his writing. Oscar was a great wit and scholar, and he was also gay. One particular young man seemed to revel in Wilde's work and celebration of men loving men. The rest of the gentlemen from the class loved to banter with him about his sexual orientation.

George

*"Dad ordered George to be normal—all the
piercings and orange hair had to go."*

Why are some men hopelessly attracted to other men? Do they choose this? If it is inherited, how do men who do not reproduce pass it on to the children they never have? My George was gay. He openly expressed his feelings for other boys, had effeminate mannerisms, was sensitive, and was a great admirer of Mr. Oscar Wilde. During "Gross Indecency" George sat next to me. I had never witnessed such intensity, as I saw that night in him. He hung on every word—it was as if the play had been written for him. During the intermission, George raved aloud at how beautiful the play was and what a marvelous job the actors were doing.

Earlier in the year, I had experienced my first close encounter with George at our fall homecoming dance. George expressed his wishes to attend, but stated that he could not afford to go. Being a faculty member, I had been invited to attend and bring a guest. And since my husband would rather stick pins in his eyes than attend a school-sponsored dance, I asked George to accompany me that year. Shortly after our arrival, he took off with the other "girls" and seemed to have a grand time.

As I began to learn the details of this young man's life, my first thoughts were that no one would ever see this story on a day-time soap opera—it was too unbelievable and sounded too phony—but it was true. Being gay was just the beginning for this youngster.

His parents came together as a miserable mismatch and produced two beautiful children, a boy and a girl. After the divorce, the children remained with mom and rarely saw dad. Mom, being a free spirit, accepted George's propensity towards other boys and openly embraced his homosexuality, as did his step-father. Unfortunately, mom's free spirit kept her from regular medical care. So she did not seek treatment for her cervical cancer until the situation was deemed hopeless.

George held her hand until the very end. He would spend hours with me describing her last hours that December. He said mom wanted people to rejoice with her and would not allow any one to cry—not even at the very end. She insisted her room be gaily decorated for Christmas and they all waved good-bye as her spirit left them.

After the funeral, George and his sister fought viciously to remain with their open-minded step-father who had reared them. But the biological dad would not hear of it. He wanted his kids; it was his right. And so they were handed over while George was a junior in high school. Dad ordered George to be normal—all the piercings and orange hair had to go. "I hate him," was all he said the first time I inquired about his father. So I decided to let it go.

George would bounce into the classroom, speak loudly to get everyone's attention, and rarely let any one get a word into the conversation. He wanted everyone to be aware of his superior intellect and knack for details, especially historical trivia. His craving for attention and monopoly of every discussion pointed to a person in need of great deal of attention.

For his senior project, George chose the topic of homosexuality. Originally I accepted his proposal of investigating how mainstream churches accepted homosexuality in their congregations. With this approach, he could separate himself from the topic while learning so much more about it. Once the project was well on its way, however, George wanted to alter his focus. He decided to attend diversity meetings, and became active at a local gay activists center. Because George was underage, I balked at changing the topic.

"You have to have your father's approval for the new topic," I informed him.

"That stupid bastard doesn't have to know anything," was his basic reply.

After I thought he doth protest too much, I called his guidance counselor for two reasons. One reason was selfish—if George did pursue the new topic, I wanted the administration to have a record of my reporting it to them. The other reason was I hoped that a new dialogue might open up among the counselor, the father, and George. I never told George he could not do the topic; I simply wanted his father involved.

His guidance counselor spoke with me on the phone and came to my room twice to discuss how to approach the subject with George.

But he never met with George. Each day I would greet George and ask, "Did you speak with your counselor?"

Every day I had the same reply, "No, haven't seen him."

After a couple of weeks, I finally typed up a memo to the counselor (with a copy to his supervisor) stating all the steps I had taken to try to get the counselor involved with George's situation—including the lack of interest and results. I told him that if he did not talk to George in one hour, I was taking the memo to the principal. Miraculously some time opened up on the busy man's schedule. He basically did nothing, other than meet with the boy.

The next step involved a student protection program at the school called SAFE. Meeting with the director, she assured me that she would find George and talk to him that day. She did, and she and George seemed to gel at first. However, when George learned that she would have to inform his father of his repeated threats to end his own life, he retaliated against her personally. She was forced to call a meeting of the downtown people, the guidance counselor, the father, and the teachers. When George's guidance counselor tried to interject his interest and compassion into the meeting, he never once had the nerve to face me. He knew that I knew that he could not be bothered—unless he was threatened.

Ultimately, George amended his project to focus on grief. He learned that much of his loathing of self and his father stemmed from his unexpressed grief. George thought that if he cried, he would be dishonoring his dear mother's last wishes. So he turned all the tears into rage, directed at the only people who cared about him.

One of our last conversations went something like this.

"If this were a perfect world, you would still have your mother to love and hold and kiss and confide in. But it's not a perfect world, and she is no longer here," I tried to explain.

So far he agreed, but he still wanted her back. He was still angry with God—or he would be if he believed in God.

"She's is not here. You do not have a mother and your sister does not have a mother. Will she be better off if she does not have a brother too?" I questioned him.

"You have the option to scream, hate, ridicule, deride, and make yourself and everyone in contact with you miserable. Or, you could look around, size up the situation, and decide how you are going to cope with it. The reality is that you have to live with your father until you go off to college. He is alive and your mom is dead. He is your father and he cares a great deal about your welfare," I continued.

George had to agree that he and his father were the worst combination of people possible on this earth—but they were blood.

"I will attempt to respect him and his ideas, at least until I no longer have to listen to him," he finally said. Did he mean it? At the time, I believed that he did. Could he pull it off? That remained to be seen. George went on to college, and someday he will be completely his own man. I hope he and dad will have a relationship—maybe not the cinema version of father and son—but at least a working relationship.

JD

So Much to Give

JD bounced into my room late with a muscle shirt on that exposed his armpits; thus, my first words to this young man were, "You cannot come in here out of dress code," so he left. He came back the next day, ready to learn, and be part of one of the most difficult classes I have ever taught.

We had everything in that 5th period English regular class. There were four who were not going to graduate because they could not pass the exit exam; next to them were five "gifted" students. The group represented every race and sexual orientation, enabling us to learn all about diversity. And we did not just learn, but loved as well. Sometimes gay men have problems with homophobic teenage boys—but this group accepted everyone.

One particularly accepting experience was our "Role Reversal Day" at school. The boys loved dressing as girls so much more than vice versa. Jonathon arrived in a pink tutu and had the class in stitches. JD's elaborate showgirl costume was fit for Broadway. He entertained and delighted everyone with his moves and female impersonator moves. They loved it. Rather than ridicule him, they joined in the fun. He was open and unabashed about being gay and the kids responded lovingly to him.

Just before his graduation, JD's guidance counselor pulled him aside at the Senior Breakfast to inform him that his community college science class "may" not count for his graduation requirements. The boy dashed into my classroom, threw himself into a desk, and wept at the thought of not walking with his class. I decided to become his advocate, because he didn't have any parents who could strong-arm the principal. I marched into the principal's office, explained the situation, and made sure that JD's credits would count. That was probably the day we bonded.

We have been in touch with each other's lives ever since. JD attends my plays where I perform in community theatre, and I visit him whenever I am able.   Now he is the youngest whale trainer in the United States. From his high school swim team dedication, to his current professional life, he brings his all—smiling and asking for nothing in return but to be himself with so much to give.

Sweet Success

"Success is counted sweetest to those who ne'r succeed"
Emily Dickenson

Is it all hopeless? Is the system overwrought with incompetents who can't pour water out of boot with the instructions written on the heel? Is the student body dominated by incorrigible criminals? Have all the decent people given up and gone home? Of course not! The system can and does work when professional, compassionate people care about their jobs. We remain teachers in spite of it all because of the successes.

I still receive Christmas cards from all over the world from former students. I am telephoned every New Year's Day by Andy who still tells me that he is almost finished with college. There were generous parents who gave me tickets for the Pistons games and beautiful Christmas baskets like the one from Jay's mom—he could hardly get it through the classroom door. I drove Latoya home from work one night when I saw her sitting on a major highway waiting for the city bus. In gratitude, she wrote the following to me on the back of her senior picture, "I know that sometimes I tend to not understand some things in life, but I want to thank you for being a good English teacher to me." My most prized school possession is a talking bear that tells me in Nikki's voice, "We'll miss you Mrs. Revell." These were all fabulous people. However, when I hear of an impossible student turning himself around—and he gives me part of the credit—that is what makes me proud to be a teacher.

Jose

From Thief to Chef

No teacher had a private office. We generally kept personal items locked away in the back, far from prying hands. One lunch hour I returned to my windowless cubby hole to find Jose rustling through some papers.

"What on earth are you doing here?" was my natural response to his intrusion.

"Mr. Chase said I should get this book for him," was Jose's glib reply, holding Dickens' *Oliver Twist* in my face.

To believe or not to believe, that was my question.

I did share office space with Mr. Chase, and the boy did seem so confident when he uttered the teacher's name. Even though all of us teachers made a pact to never allow students in the "hole," Mr. Chase often did his own thing with impunity.

Knowing I should have marched him off the dean, I decided to let him go. We only had 25 minutes for lunch and the dean was already harassing me about past discipline problems. I soon discovered that I had made a poor decision.

Jose left my office and continued down the 200 hall building, ransacking offices until he hit the jackpot. Three doors down from mine, a young teacher had left her purse in an unlocked file cabinet in an unlocked room. Jose did not leave the campus without her American Express card. He headed for local mall to purchase as much jewelry as the card could buy.

He managed to run up over $2,000 in charges before a sales clerk asked this obviously Hispanic boy why he had Lisa Deustch's credit card. Throwing the card on the counter, he fled.

When the authorities found our about my experience with Jose, I was again asked to browse through the yearbooks and try to identify him. I couldn't. Everyone looked alike to me.

This incident occurred in the spring and by the next fall, Jose was all but forgotten. Then, two weeks into the new semester a Hispanic boy strolled into my room and said, "How you doing, Mrs. Revell?" I did not click on the face, but the voice was unmistakable—it was him; it was the thief.

After class I rushed down to the main office to proudly announce that I had caught a thief. Thinking he would be hauled off to jail, I went back to class triumphantly. Jose wasn't taken anywhere. He had already been tried, convicted, placed on probation, and returned to me. I was stuck with him.

Personable in nature, but slow in the head, Jose was not such a terror—eventually I came to like him. I tried my best to give him the rudiments of an English II education and send him on his way. He never graduated, but we parted friends.

Several years later an older, flabbier, balder Jose appeared at my door in Room 211.

"Hi, Mrs. Revell. How are you?" he asked seeming quite happy with himself.

"Hi, Jose. How's life?" I replied.

"I come back to thank you," he said.

"What for?"

"For not holding my mistakes against me," he chortled.

That entire year he knew that I knew about his past, but we never spoke of it. I treated him just as I treated everyone else in the class—sans the criminal record.

"I'm married now and I have two little girls. They're so cute," he bragged as he whipped out their pictures to plant in front of my eyes.

"So, how are you supporting this young family of yours?" I asked in my best teacher voice.

"I am an assistant chef. I love it, Mrs. Revell," he patted his spreading belly and smiled, "I hope to buy my own place and be a huge success."

A "huge success" consisted of raising children and paying taxes instead of sitting in a jail cell squandering taxes—that's Jose's story.

Do I believe that I had a part in Jose's turnaround? A little. Who else helped? Everyone who came in contact with a felony-committing teenager and gave him every benefit of the doubt. Sometimes the system worked and worked well.

Omar

Dropout Makes Good

As a front seat passenger in my daughter's sports car, I was somewhat oblivious to the automobiles and people around me. I just wanted to get home from shopping and out of traffic. We had spent the afternoon at the mall and were heading home when we were stopped by a red light. I heard a horn honking, but did not look up because I knew that we were doing nothing wrong. Then I saw the arm waving, so I was certain that a tourist had lost his way and wanted to know the easiest route to the Interstate. As I rolled down my side window, my mind raced to compile the correct directions to give him.

"Aren't you Mrs. Revell?" he excitedly said.

All I could think of was that this must be how it is for real celebrities every day.

"Why, yes, I am," I answered.

"Mrs. Revell, don't you remember me? I'm Omar, Mrs. Revell, I'm Omar!" he sounded so proud.

Of course, I remembered Omar—no teacher could ever forget Omar. He was in my sophomore English class in the 1990-91 school year. How could I recall the year so vividly? Because Omar was the only student I had ever had who had been at the school all four years that it was open—yet he had accumulated only 1 credit. It was a record in the school's history. Omar never passed any of his classes, but he kept on coming to school.

When he wrote his sophomore descriptive essay in vivid detail, it landed him in the dean's office. Yes, detail was appropriate but his topic was most inappropriate. He depicted in gross detail what it was like for a dog to mount man's leg and do his thing. Only Omar would choose such a topic and invite the reader to, "picture it in your mind and describe what it sounds like, what it looks like, what it feels like, what it smells like, and what it could taste like." Oh, yes, I remembered Omar.

Although we had just a few minutes until the light turned green, Omar insisted that I meet his lovely wife and two darling children sitting in the back seat of his modest sedan. I nodded and waved, and told him that I was proud of him and the way he was caring for his young family. He beamed.

I know that I will never see Omar again, but I am so thankful that I was able to say hello that hot afternoon. I know now for myself that some children travel to a different beat, but they do not all end up in ditches with needles up their arms. Omar probably never did graduate. But he did have a wife and two children, was driving a modest style of car, and was wearing a work shirt and tie. He was smiling, proud, and good natured. He remembered his old English teacher almost ten years later, and he didn't seem to mind that I had sent him to the office for his doggy description. I'm proud of him and I am proud of me.

Snowflakes

A Sign from God

Late one May, I left school for a couple of days to attend a convention in Savannah with my husband. My daughter became a "guest teacher." Although I supplied her with detailed lessons plans for the students to accomplish in my absence, she chose to follow her own scheme. Upon my return, I entered the Room 406 to find hundreds of white, paper snowflakes hanging from the ceiling. It was breath-taking. The young people were so proud of their two days of cutting and hanging. And I loved it.

Through the years the snowflakes began to fall—some were pulled down and others fell down on their own. At one point there were a paltry six left, and they were soiled and droopy. Deserie asked me why I kept those "nasty" things in the room. I recalled that morning I walked in and saw them, bright and beautiful.

So I explained their origin to Deserie and added, "When the last of the snowflakes reaches the ground, I will take that as a sign from God that it is time for me to leave this school." She seemed to accept that explanation and never said another word to me about them.

Many months later after the seniors had graduated and were on their way, early one morning I opened my door. There hanging from the ceiling were many new beautiful snowflakes. Again I was breathless.

I closed the door, scurried to the office, and asked what had happened. I was informed that several of my seniors had returned to school after graduation and enlisted the aid of the administrators to let them into my room. They hung the snowflakes and left this message on the board:

> "These snowflakes are a gift to next year's seniors. As long as they hang, seniors, you will have the greatest English teacher ever born. You just do not know yet how lucky you are. And Mrs. Revell, please never leave—we all need you."

Teaching definitely has its own rewards.

Final Thoughts

Teachers must perceive themselves as starring in an incredibly long-running, off-off-Broadway production. Even though their "stage" is a classroom—and they have conjugated that verb thousands of times—for their students this is "opening night."

Pupils deserve all the instructor has to give in enthusiasm and attention. After decades of the same topics, this takes more and more deliberate effort. But teachers can and must replenish their energy levels to remain effective.

Students: They often face neglect and violence in their homes and neighborhoods. They need patience and personal attention. Maybe not every student, every day, gets the same dose. But certainly they should be known by name and have the teaching geared to their needs. Students really do long to have something interesting and constructive to do. Sometimes high school teens need to be persuaded that the topic has some relevance to them.

Parents: This group of people needs to be handled more gently than the students. They work hard all day, and then must deal with their teenagers in the evening. I seldom had a problem with parents when I remembered to genuinely ask for their help and assistance. Once I became an experienced "parent whisperer," I began every conversation with a compliment about their child. As long as I was sincere and specific, these little talks with parents were never wasted. Either the student responded to some direction from home, or I knew that this child was going to need an extra dose of attention at school.

Colleagues: No one does it alone; my fellow teachers offered to me the best teaching advice ever. Sharing experiences and pleading for some tips—no matter what the situation—saved me many a day. Colleges may do a great job teaching how to create lesson plans, but these plans offer a teacher little help in handling day-to-day classroom experiences. Networking within the school contributed to all that was the best in my classroom.

Administrators and Counselors: Gently pushing with a deliberate determination goes an awful long way with this group. They work with teachers—teachers do not work for them. Only with an atmosphere of cooperation on both sides does anything get done. I built strong relationships with the people that I admired the most. When I was willing to give a prize athlete extra after-school tutoring, my burned-out light bulbs were changed promptly. Coincidence, I think not.

As the saying goes, "It takes a village to raise a child," the same concept holds true for education. Working together, we can help our children to not only survive the high school jungle, but to thrive and emerge ready for the challenges of life.

Printed in the United States
139813LV00008B/145/P